THE ENGLISH FAMILY
GUIDE TO THE VENDÉE
and surrounding area

ANGELA BIRD

THE ENGLISH FAMILY GUIDE TO THE VENDÉE
and surrounding area

Illustrations by Michaël Jallier

Editions Hécate
3 bis, rue Dumaine
85400 Luçon

Thanks to John, Stella, Tom, Margaret and Annabel ; also to Josette and the many Vendean friends who have introduced us to the mysteries of their land.

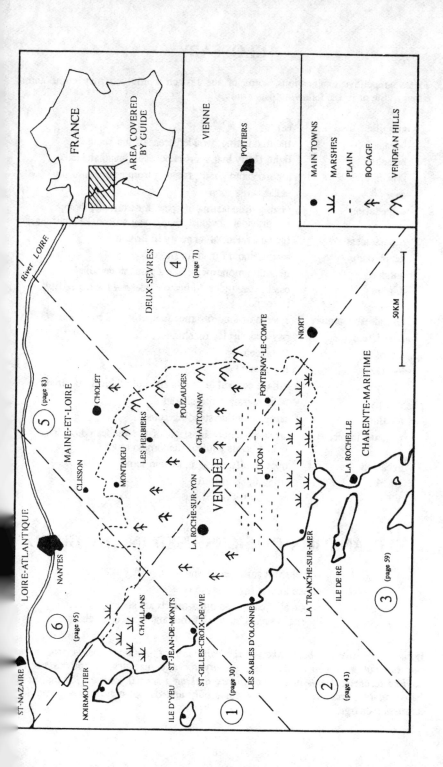

GLOSSARY

To save repetitive explanations, some of the French words you may come across either in life or in the following pages are :

anguille	eel
bocage	the undulating, wooded areas of the Vendée
brioche	light, fluffy loaf, a cross between bread and cake
brocante	second-hand goods, ranging from antiques to junk
cave	cellar, wine shop
dégustation	tasting (free tasting of wine, for example, though the provider obviously hopes you will make a purchase)
département	the equivalent of a county in Britain
dépôt-vente	second-hand furniture shop
dolmen	neolithic monument, like a giant stone table
donjon	castle keep (not a "dungeon", despite the similarity in sound)
Grande-Randonnée	system of long-distance footpaths, referred to as "GR"
horodateur	pay-and-display machine
interdit/e	forbidden
location	hire, rental
Mairie	village council office - source of all local information
marais	fens, marshes, marshland
menhir	large, neolithic standing-stone
mogette (mojette)	white haricot bean, staple of the Vendean diet ; like baked beans without the tomato sauce
occasion	opportunity, bargain, second-hand
ULM	microlight aircraft
VTT	mountain-bike

EXPLANATION OF SIGNS USED IN THE GUIDE

*	= open short summer season only
♯	= open long summer season
■	= open all year (if no other details are shown, the site is accessible at all times and there is no charge)

While every care has been taken in the compiling of this book, neither the author nor the publisher can accept responsibility for any inaccuracies and visitors are advised to check details in advance before making a special journey. Prices, usually based on 1993 rates, are given as a guide only and do not constitute a guarantee admission charge.

CONTENTS

PART I

INTRODUCTION

Nobody needs advice about how to lie and soak up the Vendée's 2,500 annual hours of sunshine on its 140km of sandy beaches. Yet inland, among the marshes, plains and rolling wooded hills is a land of ancient civilisation, legend and troubled history, visited by only a few of the half-a-million foreign tourists who arrive each year.

I have been in love with the Vendée for 25 years, slowly uncovering its mysteries and finding offbeat outings for my family. I aim to share my enjoyment and give you a taste of the towns, villages, waterways and countryside that lie beyond the campsite or the rural gîte. My guide-book will lead you slightly beyond the boundaries to places that are within easy reach for Vendée holidaymakers - you will find sorties to the north where you can visit Nantes and St-Nazaire, east to Cholet and to the state-of-the-art cinema park of Futuroscope at Poitiers, and south as far as historic La Rochelle and the Ile de Ré. I have left aside any discussion of camping establishments, hotels and restaurants, to concentrate essentially on culture and fun.

If you are staying near the seaside you will almost certainly be familiar with the "marais", the marshland dredged out of the sea by 12th-century monks and 16th-century Dutch engineers. (Squint at a present-day map through half-closed eyes and you can make out the original shoreline where the blue threads of canals meet the solid land.) You may have already crossed the patchwork of fields divided by watery ditches and canals known as the Marais Breton (famed for salt production and duck-breeding) that stretches from the mouth of the Loire southwards to St-Gilles-Croix-de-Vie. Perhaps you have glimpsed the salt-marshes north of Les Sables-d'Olonne, or the oyster-rich marshland that lies between Talmont-St-Hilaire and Jard-sur-Mer. Or maybe you know the Marais Poitevin, the flat, treeless "marais desséché" (dry marsh) south of Luçon that runs into the most famous of all - the idyllic "Venise Verte" (Green Venice), otherwise known as the "marais mouillé" (wet marsh), a network of tree-lined, duckweed-covered waterways that reaches towards Niort.

The "bocage" covers most of the rest - the "haut-bocage" being the wooded, comparatively hilly area down the eastern fringe of the "département" (county), and the "bas-bocage" the gently undulating land that surrounds La Roche-sur-Yon and continues towards the coast. This area is dotted with small farmhouses and cottages - their doorways often outlined in white and topped by a cross in white paint to keep out witches and ill-fortune. Neolithic man built dolmens and raised the enormous standing-stones known as menhirs here and more than 4000 years later, after the French Revolution, 18th-century guerrillas hid in the forests to escape the flames guns and bayonets of the Republican troops.

Blending into the Marais Poitevin and the bocage is the "plaine", a series of vast rolling prairies that stretches between Ste-Hermine and Fontenay-le-Comte and which provide the Vendée's cereal crops of maize, wheat and sunflowers. The red roofed houses here exude prosperity - tall and substantial, they are built of fine, white stone, unlike the ground-hugging, whitewashed cottages of the marshes.

I shall not linger on the coast, except to suggest some of its alternative attractions and to recommend serious seaside-lovers to obtain tide-tables ("horaires des marées") free from tourist offices. In July and August the sands are often extremely crowded and the smarter town beaches like those of Les Sables-d'Olonne and St-Gilles-Croix-de-Vie can become unbearably congested at high tide ("pleine mer"), particularly where this occurs in mid-afternoon. Holidaymakers get concentrated ever closer to the sea wall, and a bit of research pays off if you want to avoid the crush. Just aim for the period around "basse mer" (low tide) to enjoy the maximum personal space.

For a bit of variety, get out a good map and head inland ; there you can walk in the forests, rent a mountain-bike, look for dolmens and canoe through the marshes, or admire the Vendée's rich legacy of ninth- to 13th-century Romanesque architecture, ride on a steam train, go birdwatching or visit a submarine. And, if you are unfortunate enough to wake up to a spot of rain, you can dip into this book to find museums, castles, aquariums and "brocantes" (junk shops) in which to while away the time until the sun comes out again. I have included an at-a-glance indication of opening periods to help out-of-season visitors home in easily on what to do in autumn, winter and spring, as well as high summer.

Sports-lovers and night-owls will have no difficulty discovering riding establishments, casinos and discos, which are well documented in tourist offices, but I have attempted here to point out some of the Vendée's other resources - unusual museums, rural events and market-days - and to throw in a seasoning of things that I, personally, find irresistible on holiday like flea markets, crafts fairs, and getting acquainted with local customs and food - you haven't lived until you've tried the region's ham and "mogettes" (white haricot beans), barbecued quail, grilled sardines, eels cooked over cowpat fires, or fried ostrich.

Village festivals (heavily advertised on posters and banners throughout the neighbourhood) are great fun. They usually take place on a Sunday and tend to promote different local traditions from oyster-fishing to the baking of brioches. Bonfires are often lit to celebrate the Feast of St John the Baptist around 24 June, which makes a further excuse for festivities. The Fête Nationale (Bastille Day) is marked by parades and fireworks on the evening of either 13 or 14 July, though events are sometimes low-key in this region which was decidedly anti-Republican after the 1789 Revolution. The circus remains a much-loved tradition in France, and travelling companies still pitch their tents in the holiday towns and villages. The biggest are Amar, Pindar, Bouglione and Zavatta, though many other tiny ones pop up in seaside car-parks and village squares. In mid-September a weekend of "journées du patrimoine" (National Heritage Days) gives you a chance to visit around 30 properties that are normally closed to the public - you can pick up a brochure from tourist offices during the few weeks beforehand. From mid-September to mid-January is the eagerly-awaited season for "la chasse" (shooting). On Sundays (and on one other day, that varies from village to village) the locals pick up their guns and lurk among the hedgerows from dawn to dusk, firing at anything from rabbits to wild boar, so it is probably wise to resist taking country walks on those days if you want to avoid being peppered with shot. However, if the autumn sunshine is too tempting, at least make sure you are noticed by wearing something brightly-coloured.

The heritage has its melancholy side, too. Western France was torn by the Hundred Years' War (against the English) and the Wars of Religion (that pitched Catholics against Protestants). But the region suffered most cruelly during the Wars of the Vendée, a bitter civil war waged by the strongly Catholic Vendean peasants (who supported the exiled French monarchy) against the Republicans' new ideas and well-armed forces immediately after the French Revolution of 1789. If you want to understand the soul of the region you should skim through the section on pages 24 to 28 which sets out the highlights of this long struggle which is indelibly stamped on the Vendean collective memory. In just three years from March 1793 the uprising cost between 250,000 and 300,000 lives. Almost every village was destroyed, castles and manor houses were reduced to ruins, and a ruthless policy of extermination reduced the population by one third - in certain villages by up to a half. So it is no surprise that most pre-19th-century castles, houses and churches are in various stages of ruination - the miracle is that any are left at all.

Since those days the Vendean emblem, which you will come across everywhere, is of two intertwined hearts topped with a cross and a crown to symbolise the region's twin loyalties to church and king.

For long a quiet agricultural and fishing backwater, the Vendée has recently surged ahead into intensive farming and fish-breeding, a new way of life that is enthusiastically shared with visitors, who are welcomed to fishing trawlers, to farms raising shellfish, deer, bison, snails and eels, and to one of France's largest national studs. The département has begun, in the nick of time, to rescue its heritage of crumbling Romanesque churches, feudal strongholds and Renaissance castles from layers of ivy and centuries of neglect. Houses connected with local celebrities like politician Georges Clemenceau, painter Charles Milcendeau and military hero Marshal Jean de Lattre de Tassigny give fascinating insights into provincial French life. No less intriguing are the museums that have evolved from the passions of private collectors, whether of prams, dolls, model vehicles, stuffed animals, or vintage cars.

I have given titles of museums and other events in French, since this is how you will see them advertised or signposted. Most of the smaller establishments have tours and details only in French, so I have tried to explain enough historical background to give non-French-speakers a little understanding of displays or events. The cut-off point for children's admission rates varies between about 12 and 16 years and, if anyone in your party is aged over 60, it is worth enquiring about a similar reduction for "troisième-âge". Opening details may be varied on public holidays (see page 18).

I wish you a wonderful, interest-filled holiday, though I am certain you will find - as I have, even after 25 years of Vendée summers - that it will not be long enough.

USEFUL INFORMATION

BOATING

Canoeing
Guided tours through open marshland at Sallertaine, St-Jean-de-Monts, Bois-de-Céné, or on the river Vie at Apremont.

Trips through open landscape surrounding the river Tenu near Port-St-Père.

Signposted routes through the Marais Poitevin (Green Venice) from Damvix Maillezais, Magné, Coulon, Bessines, Arçais, La Garette and La Ronde.

Canoes for rent also on the Vendée's many large inland lakes.

Traditional craft
Le Marais Poitevin (Green Venice) : paddle a flat-bottomed "plate" (or be conducted by a boatman) through tree-lined waterways from Coulon, Maillezais, Damvix Maillé, Le Mazeau.

Parc Régional de la Grande Brière (Loire-Atlantique) : guided tours of this marshland national park by traditional boat known as a "chaland" from Fédrun, Bréca, L Chaussée Neuve, Rozé, Kerfeuille and Le Clos d'Orange.

CYCLING

For cycle hire ("location de vélos"), enquire at tourist offices or railway stations. Many local trails are signposted.

Guided tours are available of the Marais Breton - the open marshland near Challans - by VTT (mountain-bike) from Sallertaine ; other guided trips are offered through the marshland and countryside surrounding Les Sables-d'Olonne (mountain-bikes provided in both cases).

Sections of an Atlantic cycleway, which will eventually run the whole length of the Vendée's 250km coastline, are opening in stages from 1994.

ELECTRICITY

The electric current is usually 220v, so British equipment should function perfectly successfully if you have brought the appropriate travel adaptor to convert your plug to fit a French socket. These are widely available in British shops, and also on ferries and at airports.

ENTERTAINMENT

Theatres

There is one theatre at La Roche-sur-Yon and another at Fontenay-le-Comte. Outside the département you will find theatres at La Rochelle and Nantes (where opera performances are also given at the Théâtre Graslin between October and June). It is usual to tip the usherette who shows you to your seat - about 1F should do.

Cinemas

The French are great movie-goers and most towns, even quite small ones, have cinemas. In addition, some village halls have monthly screenings of "family" films during the winter months. Performance times are usually given in the local newspapers such as "Vendée-Matin" or "Ouest-France" (be sure you have picked up the appropriate edition - if you buy a copy at some distance from your base you are apt to find it covers different towns entirely from the ones you are interested in). Have a 1F piece ready to slip to the usherette if you are shown to your seat. With the exception of showings in a few Nantes cinemas, films will always be in French - English-language ones will be dubbed, not subtitled, so entertainment value for non-French-speakers is limited. (See "v o" below.)

Television

If you should have access to a television set, you will normally receive TF1, France 2, France 3, Arte and M6. A cable channel, Canal+, is often piped into hotels. Many English or American films and series fill the airwaves, but almost all will be dubbed into French unless you see the magic letters "v o" beside them in the newspaper or TV guide. These stand for "version originale" and indicate that the film is shown in its original language, with French subtitles. Of course this is not much help if the film was Swedish or German in the first place...

TF1 is a populist channel, showing many game and variety shows. France 2 is a little like BBC2, with more serious and cultural subjects. France 3 has a local bias and, at about 7.30pm in the summer months, shows a daily briefing in English of regional forthcoming events for tourists ; it also shows early-morning and late-night round-ups of news from different European countries three times a week. Arte is a Franco-German channel that quite often has quirky English programmes like "Monty Python's Flying Circus" and "The New Statesman" in "v o". M6 is heavily pop-oriented. Canal+ ("Canal Plus") shows mainly cinema films - some late-night ones in "v o".

Radio

French radio channels include the local Vendean "Alouette fm" on 92.8Mhz which has a tourist round-up each day in summer at 10-11am and 3-4pm (with parts of the broadcast in English, as well as French and German). You can usually pick up BBC Radio 4 (200kHz/1500m long wave) and, of course, the BBC World Service.

FISHING

Freshwater fishing

A 10-day licence to fish ("Carte Pêche Vacances") in all non-private waterways of the Vendée, obtainable between 1 June and 31 August, costs around 120F. Information from Mairies and tourist offices, or from La Fédération de Pêche de Vendée, 10bis Rue Haxo, BP 673, 85016 La Roche-sur-Yon Cedex (tel : 51 37 19 05). Always ask before fishing, if in any doubt about whether a stretch of water is included in the pass ("Pêche Interdite" means No Fishing). Note that if you want to fish in a neighbouring département you need to obtain a different pass to cover the new area.

Traditional fishing

Annual event on 15 August and the first Sunday after, at Passay on the lake of St-Philbert-de-Grand-Lieu (Loire-Atlantique, south of Nantes). On these two days you can help fishermen haul in the long seine nets, but be prepared to wade through the mud and reeds.

Sea fishing

Boat trips may be taken from Les Sables-d'Olonne of two and four hours' duration, or you can go out on a real trawler and watch other people fish for a living. Sea-fishing trips are also available from St-Gilles-Croix-de-Vie.

Shrimping and shellfish-collecting

Wade in the shallows and the rock-pools at low tide with a shrimping net ; join the locals digging for shellfish at extra-low water on sandy beaches, or alongside the causeway leading to the island of Noirmoutier (consult tide-tables to find the days with the highest coefficients). Keep an eye on the incoming tide, though, and stay well away from any commercial oyster-beds or mussel-posts.

FOOD

Traditional local specialities are hearty, peasant food like cabbage, and the white haricot beans known as "mogettes" - also sometimes written "mojettes" - which could be simmered slowly in the embers of the fire while everybody toiled in the fields. With such a long coastline and active fishing industry, fish and shellfish are an important part of the repertoire, especially mussels from L'Aiguillon-sur-Mer, oysters from the bay of Bourgneuf, sardines from St-Gilles-Croix-de-Vie and sole from Les Sables-d'Olonne.

Shellfish

When you buy fish and shellfish in a shop, don't hesitate to ask for advice on cooking them. Shrimps and prawns are usually sold cooked (the little brown shrimps known as "crevette grises" have much more flavour than their pretty pink cousins). Langoustines can be ready-cooked ("cuites") or raw ("crues") - if uncooked they should be plunged into a large saucepan of well-salted boiling water, flavoured with pepper and a little vinegar, and cooked for just two minutes once the water has returned to the boil. Then run them under cold water to cool rapidly.

Crabs can be bought cooked, but most often are still clambering over one another, blowing bubbles, in the fishmonger's tray. The non-squeamish can steel themselves to place the creature in a large saucepan of cold water, heavily salted and flavoured with pepper and a bouquet-garni of available herbs, bringing it to the boil and cooking for 12 minutes per kilo (about six minutes per pound). Plunge the crab into cold water immediately it is cooked. The only parts you should not eat are the fleshy, grey, finger-shaped gills and the stringy intestine. A pair of nutcrackers (or pliers, hammer, or even, at a pinch, a couple of good, flat stones) is invaluable for smashing your way into the better-protected parts - try to buy some pointed, metal shellfish-picks in a supermarket to fish out the best bits. Spider crabs ("araignées") should be put into boiling water flavoured with a little cayenne pepper and cooked for 20 minutes per kilo (about 10 minutes per pound), then allowed to cool in the cooking water. (You can always order cooked crabs or lobsters from a fishmonger, at a day's notice.)

Mussels and other shellfish need to be well scrubbed and scraped, using a sharp knife to remove barnacles and also any whiskery bits of "beard". Discard any that are not tightly closed. You can sometimes buy ready-scraped mussels ("moules grattées") which saves you a bit of work, but you should still look them over carefully. To cook a kilo of mussels, heat 125ml of Muscadet, Gros-Plant or other dry white wine with a chopped onion, a chopped clove of garlic, 2 tsp of chopped parsley and seasoning. When it is boiling, add the mussels, cover the pan and steam for five to 10 minutes until they are all open. Stir a little butter or cream into the juice before pouring it over them. You can do something similar with cockles ("coques") and other shellfish, though the French prefer them eaten raw. Oysters - usually the long, lumpy "portugaise" variety - in season all year round are, to English minds, incredibly inexpensive, and just require opening before serving. You can buy cheap, stubby blades with a special shield around the handle from hardware shops or supermarkets, which you use to attack the hinged end of the creature, avoiding getting flakes of shell mingled with the delicate flesh. First, however, wrap your other hand in a tea-towel for protection, should the knife slip. If you are going to make a habit of opening them, you may want to treat yourself to an electric, vibrating, oyster-knife.

Fish

Fresh sardines are a real, yet inexpensive, treat. Gut and wash them well. For barbecuing it is easiest to cook them in a metal, double tennis-racquet arrangement if you can lay your hands on one. Sprinkle them with olive oil and some coarse Noirmoutier sea-salt first and grill for about three minutes each side (depending on thickness). Eat with something plain, like boiled potatoes or crusty bread, and butter. You can also barbecue steaks of fresh tuna ("thon"). The red-tinged meat is very filling, and particularly delicious with a horseradish and cream sauce - if you are British enough to have brought horseradish with you. A wonderful fish soup in large glass jars is sold in shops and supermarkets under the label of "La Vendéenne".

Vegetables

Mogettes (haricot beans), introduced to the area by monks in the 16th century after Pope Clement VII had been presented with some from South America, need to be soaked overnight before cooking, and then simmered for an hour or two in water with no salt, just bouquet garni. Salt them only *after* they are cooked. You can stir in some "crème fraîche" (slightly soured cream) after draining them. (If you can't be bothered with all this, there is an excellent, home-cooked version available in supermarkets under the "Recettes d'Autrefois" label.) The beans - also known as "lingots" - are traditionally served with ham ("jambon"), another Vendean speciality, cured using a mixture of sea salt, spices and eau-de-vie. In late summer you sometimes see the new season's beans, called "demi-secs", on sale still in their withered pods ; these need no soaking before they are cooked.

If you find strange mushrooms irresistible, you can take any that you gather in forests and hedgerows to a chemist for identification and advice about whether they can be eaten. On the whole it is probably safer to stick with those you can buy in the markets around October ; chanterelles, ceps and horns of plenty ("trompettes de la mort") look quite adventurous enough for most people.

Sea salt, grey and chunky, known as "sel de mer" or "gros-sel" made the fortunes of the monasteries in the Middle Ages since it was in demand everywhere for the preservation of food. Today it is still made, on a smaller scale, with the same techniques in the salt marshes of Guérande, Noirmoutier and Olonne-sur-Mer, and makes interesting (and comparatively cheap) presents for foodie friends back home. Also grown in the same marshes and becoming more available is the red, fleshy-leaved samphire ("salicorne") that turns green when cooked and is sold, pickled, as a condiment, or fresh for brief cooking and using as a vegetable or in a salad.

The island of Noirmoutier enjoys a microclimate that enables it to produce the first French new potatoes of the year - rather like Jersey Royals for the British - as early as February. The delicious, fresh taste in early spring is compensation for the slightly sorry sight of the island's fields under plastic wraps through the winter.

Poultry and meat

One of the region's most important agricultural products today is poultry. Chicken and duck are familiar enough ; guinea-fowl ("pintade") can be cooked like chicken ; quail ("caille") - of which you need one or two per person - may be roasted or casseroled for about 20 minutes, and needs extra flavour from added bits of bacon,

Muscadet, Pineau, grapes, etc. Beautiful, speckled quail's eggs make an attractive starter when hard-boiled (cook for about four minutes, and cool rapidly under cold water) and served with dips of salt or mayonnaise. You can also barbecue quail, in which case it is best to split the birds down the backbone, open them out and then marinate them for a few hours in a tasty combination of herbs, oil, onions and other flavourings.

Meat is often sold in boned and rolled joints which make carving a real pleasure. If you have a barbecue with a battery-operated spit, try doing a piece of beef ("rôti de boeuf"), studded with a few cloves of garlic if you like. It doesn't take long to cook - about 20 to 30 minutes, depending on thickness - and, though it is not cheap, there is no waste ; in the unlikely event of any being left over, it is even better cold.

Cheese

Many craftsman-made cheeses can be found in the market-halls in Vendean towns and villages, and some of the smaller specialists - mostly goat's-cheese producers - encourage visitors to stop at their "fromageries" where you can see the process and sample different types of cheese.

Desserts

For the sweet-toothed, there is quite a choice. The Vendée is known for its impossibly light, fluffy loaves of brioche (a sweet bread made of eggs, flour, sugar, yeast, salt, butter and milk, plus a dash of rum or of orange-flower water) that was traditionally made as an Easter speciality, and is still served at midnight, with coffee, at local weddings. Every village has its own variety, though it is said to originate in Vendrennes, near Les Herbiers. Other treats include "flan maraîchin" (a pastry case holding an egg custard), "tourteau au fromage" (a black-domed cheesecake, made from goat's cheese, nestling in a pastry case), "fouace" or "fouasse" (a cross between cake and bread, more sustaining and compact in texture than brioche), and a delicious ice-cream confection bearing the Vendée's hearts-and-crown logo, the "R'tournez'y", that mingles vanilla, hazelnut and wild strawberry to brilliant effect, and is packed for you in an insulated container so you can keep it cold long enough to get home and enjoy it.

GOLF

Vendée Golf Pass

A season ticket is available, valid for one month, covering five 18-hole, par-72 courses : 1 July-31 Aug, 950F ; 1 September-30 June, 600F This entitles you to one round on each, plus 20% discount on further green fees. Golf clubs may be hired for around 50F a round. Information and reservations : Club des Golfs de Vendée, Club House, Golf des Fontenelles, 85220 L'Aiguillon-sur-Vie (tel : 51 54 57 57 ; fax : 51 55 45 77) ; British reservation centre: David Moore Consultancy, 182-194 Union Street, London SE1 0LH (tel : 071-928 2344 ; fax : 071-620 0304). The courses are at St-Jean-de-Monts, L'Aiguillon-sur-Vie (near Coëx), Nesmy (near La Roche-sur-Yon), Les Sables-d'Olonne, and Port-Bourgenay (near Talmont-St-Hilaire). A handicap of 36 or less is normally required ; between May and September it is best to book in advance on the more popular courses like St-Jean-de-Monts and Port-Bourgenay.

Swin-Golf

This is not a misprint but a new sport, using just one club with three different faces to take the place of a normal bagful. Courses consist of nine or 18 holes, and are appearing in more places by the moment.

Mini-Golf
Great fun for all the family, these nine- or 18-hole circuits with jokey hazards built into them will entertain everyone from six-year-olds to grandparents.

HOTELS AND RESTAURANTS
Good reference books are the Michelin red guide or the Logis de France book for both hotels and restaurants - Michelin awards up to three stars for gastronomic excellence ; the Logis awards casseroles. Restaurant guides include the Gault-Millau (which accords marks out of 20), and the Guide des Relais Routiers for good-value, meals. Some of the best - though relatively expensive - places to eat in the Vendée feature in "Les Toques Vendéennes", a booklet available from tourist offices and quality food shops. You can often eat well and cheaply at small, family-run establishments - look around a market-square, for example, or ask the locals for advice. To rent a gîte, or holiday cottage, you should contact the French Government Tourist Office, 178 Piccadilly, London W1V 9DB, or make a direct approach to the tourist office in the French town nearest to your preferred area.

MAPS
You need good maps to get the most out of a holiday. The familiar, yellow-backed Michelin series is excellent and, at around 10F, good value. Even better - though more expensive - are the IGN (Institut Géographique National) green series on the scale of 1cm = 1km - either No 32 (Nantes/Les Sables-d'Olonne) or No 33 (Cholet/Niort), depending on where you are based. For even more detail on an area you want to walk or explore in depth, nothing beats the IGN blue series where 4cm = 1km. The IGN also produces a red series at 1cm = 2.5km, of which No 107 covers Poitou-Charentes from St-Nazaire to Royan and Tours to Limoges. It marks some tourist attractions but is by no means comprehensive, though it has a useful gazetteer on the back and its scope makes it handy if you are touring by car over a wide area.

MEASUREMENTS
All indications of distance, area and weight in this guide are metric.
> 1kg = 2.2lb
> 500g = 1.1lb (also often called "une livre")
> 1litre = 1.75pt (1 gallon = 4.54litres)
> 1km = 0.6 miles (1 mile = 1.6km)
> 1 hectare = 2.47 acres (260 hectares = 1 square mile)

MEDICAL EXPENSES
If you hold a form E111 (obtainable over the counter in British post offices), you can claim some reimbursement of medical expenses under the reciprocal arrangement between Britain and France. After consulting (and paying) the doctor or dentist, take the "feuille de soins" (medical treatment form) that you are given and hand it to the chemist with your "ordonnance" (prescription) form. The chemist dispenses the drugs (it is most important to keep any sticky labels from the boxes), and adds their details to the form. Take or send the form and sticky labels, with your E111 and the passport (or a photocopy of its important pages, if you are posting it) relating to the person in whose name the E111 is issued, to the nearest Caisse Primaire Assurance Maladie - there is one at Immeuble du Dispensaire, Boulevard René Bazin, 85300

Challans (tel : 51 49 38 83), and another at Rue Alain (off the eastern end of Boulevard des États-Unis), 85000 La Roche-sur-Yon (tel : 51 44 16 16). You should get quite a large percentage of your costs reimbursed, though it will take them around six weeks to send you the cheque.

Chemists are often consulted about minor ailments and discuss them with doctor-like gravity, binding up sprained ankles and dishing out reasonably strong medicines without the need for getting into the intricacies of the French health system. You do not, however, get reimbursed for this treatment.

MONEY

In towns and large villages banks are usually open from Monday to Friday, or Tuesday to Saturday, from 9am-noon and 2pm until about 6pm. It is important to note, however, that they close for public holidays from lunch-time the previous day which can catch you unawares, and that if the holiday falls on a Tuesday or a Thursday there is a tendency to join the day up to the nearest weekend ("faire le pont") and close for several days at a stretch. (See Public Holidays, page 18)

However, if you have the sort of bank card that extracts cash from a hole in the wall in England, the chances are that it will work in France, as long as it has a similar logo on it - i.e. Visa, MasterCard, etc - to that displayed on the French cash machine. Crédit Mutuel, Crédit Lyonnais and Crédit Agricole cash-dispensers have on-screen instructions in English as well as French. You have to use a second set of keys (with pre-set amounts like 500F or 1000F) to enter the amount to be withdrawn, rather than typing it on the same set of keys that you used to enter your PIN. Of course, you can also draw cash on Visa or Access credit cards if you have a PIN for those, but that is a more expensive solution than bank cards as you have to pay interest on credit-card cash advances right away. Credit cards like Access, Visa, American Express and Diner's Club are widely accepted, particularly the first two, and can be used at petrol stations, supermarkets, hotels, restaurants and shops (except, of course, small village shops, restaurants and cafés). Cards in France are more sophisticated than British ones, and allow the cardholder to tap in a secret authorisation code on a T-shaped keyboard. The British cards still require you to sign for the goods you buy, and you may need to remind the shopkeeper of this if he/she offers you the keyboard to punch. You are often asked for your passport when cashing travellers' cheques or Eurocheques in a bank, so it is as well to take it with you.

MOTORING

You should always have the car's documents - original of log-book (plus letter of authorisation from the vehicle's owner if it is not registered in your name), green card or insurance certificate, and your driving-licence - with you in the vehicle when you are driving it. You can be stopped at any time for spot checks, and it is an offence to be without them. (Major roads are particularly heavily policed around 5pm each day and on Sunday afternoons.) On-the-spot fines are common ; speeding penalties start at around 1,100F (approximately £140). All front- and rear-seat passengers must wear seat belts. Drink/drive limits are broadly similar to those operating in England and random breath tests can be carried out. You should carry a warning triangle for use if your car breaks down, and a spare set of bulbs for your lights (it is an offence to drive with any light out of order).

Note that if a French driver flashes headlights at you he is not giving you the right of way - he is announcing that he is taking it for himself.

Speed limits

130kph/81mph on motorways (110kph/68mph in bad conditions).
110kph/68mph on dual carriageways (100kph/62mph in bad conditions).
90kph/56mph on other roads (80kph/50mph in bad conditions).
50kph/31mph in towns and villages (unless marked otherwise) from the moment you have passed the village's name-board, until you pass the crossed-out name on the way out - even if no speed limit is marked). The limit does not apply to hamlets whose names appear only on a very small sign.
In conditions where visibility is reduced to 50m, limits everywhere are 50kph.

Parking

Meters do not need much explanation, except to say look closely at the times and days. There is often a free period that covers protracted French lunchtimes in inland towns, and at seaside resorts Sundays and public holidays usually still require payment. In streets and car parks the system is often one of pay-and-display ("horodateur" or "distributeur") - again, look carefully to see exactly what hours and days require payment. The third, and oldest-established, method of parking regulation is by parking disc in areas designated as "zones bleues" by street signs or by painted blue marks on the road. If you do not already own a parking disc ("disque de contrôle de stationnement"), you can usually buy one at a nearby stationer's.

NEWSPAPERS

One-day-old English newspapers are widely available in good newsagents/bookshops like Maisons de la Presse, though without any colour magazine sections. The two local newspapers are "Ouest-France" (which enjoys much the larger circulation) and "Vendée-Matin", both of which appear Monday to Saturday. They carry some international and national news, and invaluable pages of local snippets to interest the French-reading holidaymaker, such as cinema and exhibition listings, details of local fêtes, scandals, accidents and other indispensable trivia.

POST OFFICES

Main offices are open Monday to Friday 8am-7pm ; Saturday 8am until noon. However, outside La Roche-sur-Yon and large cities like Nantes they close from noon until 2pm for lunch. You can send faxes ("télécopies") from the larger post offices, and consult their phone books or Minitel machines (computerised telephone directories).

PUBLIC HOLIDAYS

Public holidays are : 1 January, Easter Monday (lundi de Pâques), 1 May, 8 May (VE Day 1945), Ascension Day, Whit Monday (lundi de Pentecôte), 14 July, 15 August (l'Assomption), 1 November (la Toussaint), 11 November (Armistice 1918), 25 December.

RIDING

There are many equestrian centres ("centres équestres") in the region - enquire through local tourist offices. Note that establishments may not all provide hard hats ("bombes" in French), so it is as well to check this point first if you have not brought your own.

SAFETY

Safety norms tend not to be as stringent as in England ; you will probably notice a lack of lifejackets, riding-hats and safety barriers, and that amusement park rides seem a bit more perilous than you are used to.

SHOPPING

The lunch hour is sacrosanct in France, and most shops - apart from the large hypermarkets - close between noon and 2pm. Consequently, the lie-a-bed holidaymaker will find the mornings extremely short for shopping but, in contrast, the afternoons deliciously long as shops generally stay open until around 7pm. In summer, however, some of the medium-sized supermarkets in holiday areas remain open at lunchtime, and may also trade on Sunday mornings. Markets usually operate in the mornings, up to about noon. Local food shops are open on Sunday mornings.

STAR-GAZING

If you are staying somewhere far from street-lighting, under night skies that are really dark, the planets and the constellations stand out wonderfully. In mid-August you may also spot shooting-stars zipping across the heavens.

TELEPHONES

Telephone cabins, as in England, come in two varieties - those that take cash and those that take cards ("télécartes") which can be purchased at post offices and "tabacs" or tobacconists. If you want to make a reversed-charge call ("une communication en PCV") or to have somebody call you back in a call-box, look around first to find the number, which should be printed somewhere on the wall inside the cabin. French numbers are quoted in pairs - 12 34 56 78 would be "douze, trente-quatre, cinquante-six, soixante-dix-huit", so you need to practise that first before telling the operator.) To make a transfer charge call to Great Britain you should dial 19 00 44 to get an English-speaking operator.

To call a number in Britain direct, first dial 19, wait for a new tone, then dial 44, followed by the British number you require, but omitting the zero at the beginning. To call another number in France, you just dial the eight figures of the number, unless it is in Paris or the Paris region, in which case you must dial 16 first, wait for the new tone, then dial 1, followed by the eight-figure number.

Cheap-rate time for calls to England is Monday to Friday from 9.30pm, Saturdays from 2pm, Sundays and French bank holidays all day.

Emergency numbers:

Fire (Pompiers)	18
Police (Police in towns ; gendarmerie in rural areas)	17
SAMU (Paramedics)	15
Operator (Opérateur)	13
Directory enquiries (Renseignements)	12
(for overseas directory enquiries dial 19 33 12	
+ country identification no - i.e. 44 for UK)	

You can call up the recorded weather forecast for the département on 36 65 02 85, or for the Vendean seaside on 36 65 08 85.

Although all Vendée telephone subscribers' numbers fit into a single telephone directory, you need to know which town or village someone lives in before looking them up, as entries are listed under localities. This can be a problem if the person you are calling lives in an isolated country house or a small hamlet - you have to know the name of the commune (the larger village under which it falls administratively) to be able to find the entry you want.

TENNIS

Most villages have a municipal tennis court or two, which can be booked by the hour, for a modest fee, a day or so in advance. Ask at the Mairie.

TIPPING

Strictly speaking, service is now included in the bill for bars, hotels and restaurants, and indicated by the words "prix nets". However, it is usual to leave something extra, even if it is just the bits of loose change on the plate - especially if service was particularly good or if you are likely to return. It is customary to tip usherettes in theatre or cinema, if they show you to your seat - about 1F ; hairdressers and taxi-drivers about 10 per cent of the bill ; and a few francs to a guide after a tour of some interesting place.

WALKING

Grande-Randonnée

The IGN map 903 shows all the Grande-Randonnée (long-distance footpath) routes in France; "topo-guides" (special large-scale maps) describing the various walks in detail are obtainable from good bookshops. Grande-Randonnée footpaths in the Vendée, marked with red-and-yellow signs, include GR36, GR364, GR Pays Entre Vie et Yon and GR Pays de la Côte de Lumière. You can, of course, walk short sections of them. Maps of local walks are often available from tourist offices, otherwise consult the Comité Départemental de la Randonnée Pédestre, Bâtiment F, La Vigne-aux-Roses, 85000 La Roche-sur-Yon (tel : 51 05 37 05), or the Fédération Française de la Randonnée Pédestre, 24 Rue de la Montparière, 85170 Le Poiré-sur-Vie (tel : 51 31 87 71).

Chemin de St-Jacques-de-Compostelle

A new system of signposted trails is being set up, to guide walkers in the footsteps of the 11th-century pilgrims who journeyed through Europe to the shrine of St James the elder at Santiago de Compostela in north-west Spain. From Brittany, Britain and Scandinavia, they followed routes - now half-forgotten bridlepaths and sunken lanes - many of which passed through the Vendée. Hostel accommodation and further information at the village of Palluau (see page 52).

Local walks

Almost every village has signposted footpaths leading to its main beauty spots and places of interest. Information is sometimes given on large panels in village car parks or may be obtained from local tourist offices or Mairies.

WILDLIFE

Among bird-life, hoopoes and buzzards are not uncommon, and swallowtail butter-flies a far more usual sight than they are in Britain. At twilight you may sense the occasional bat swooping overhead or, once darkness falls, spy glow-worms as pinpricks of bright neon in the hedgerows and grass verges. Mosquitoes and other insects are not particularly troublesome, though the wasp-like "frelons" (hornets) can give a nasty sting. As in Britain, the only poisonous snake is the "vipère" or adder, a y creature that might bask on sunny heathland but will beat a rapid retreat if it nses you coming.

VINES

esides the celebrated Muscadet - made from a Burgundy grape variety called Melon" - and the even drier Gros-Plant derived from the Folle-Blanche grape, which e grown on the northern limits of the département, the Vendée has four wine-owing areas producing a series of unpretentious reds, whites and rosés which have rned VDQS status). These wines, produced at Brem-sur-Mer, at Mareuil-sur-le-Lay d neighbouring Rosnay, at Vix, and at the aptly-named Pissotte and marketed der the Fiefs Vendéens label have a long history. Known to the Romans, they were aaffed by the 16th-century writer Rabelais and, later, served at the table of Cardinal ichelieu when he was bishop of Luçon.

here is a museum of wine-making techniques at Brem, and welcoming vineyards each area at which you can taste the output. The small village of Rosnay has 44 oducers among a population of just over 450 - said to be a record, even for France. he main categories of wine quality, in descending order, are : AOC (Appellation Origine Contrôlée), accorded to the region's three types of Muscadet - the ordinary rsion, the Muscadet de Sèvre-et-Maine, and Muscadet des Coteaux de la Loire ; DQS (Vin Délimité de Qualité Supérieure), accorded to Gros-Plant and Fiefs endéens wines, and also to the reds, rosés and whites produced in the Coteaux Ancenis area alongside the Loire to the west of Nantes ; Vin de Pays, denoting a ugher table wine ; and Vin de Table, covering the rest. he finest of the local wines is Muscadet de Sèvre-et-Maine (produced to the east of antes), particularly that which is bottled "sur-lie" - left for longer in the barrel on e lees, or sediment, to acquire a slightly sparkling quality. In the heart of the luscadet area, south-east of Nantes, you will find museums of wine at Le Pallet and at La Haye-Fouassière. Stronger local specialities include Pineau-des-Charentes - a delicious fortified wine made from Charente grape-juice blended with cognac, that comes in white or rosé versions and is widely available to be drunk, chilled, as an apéritif ; a coffee-based liqueur called Kamok, made since 1812 in Luçon ; and Séguin, a brandy-type drink, distilled at Machecoul from wines of the Loire.

Further information

Maps and more details on all the above may be obtained from local tourist offices in towns, or from the Mairie in villages (these establishments are usually open Monday to Friday in the mornings).

A LITTLE FRENCH HISTORY

You will probably decide that the last thing you want on holiday is a history lesson. Nevertheless, there may come a moment when you want to understand more of the Vendée wars, for example, or to remember which British historical periods coincided with which French ones. Here are some historical landmarks, with a few notes about architectural styles, plus a potted history of events in the Vendée.

Date	French history	Corresponding British history
7500-2500BC	Neolithic period (dolmens, menhirs).	Neolithic period.
4th century AD	Christianity reaches Poitou.	Christianity reaches Britain.
MIDDLE AGES		
AD486	Beginning of Mérovingian period.	Anglo-Saxon.
751	Beginning of Carolingian period.	Saxon kingdoms.
987	Beginning of Capetian period. (Romanesque architecture, 10th-12th century - pilgrims.)	Ethelred II (Saxon) then Danes, Saxons and Normans.
1152	Henri Plantagenêt (Henry II of England) marries Eleanor of Aquitaine. (Gothic architecture, 12th-15th centuries.)	From 1154 Henry II (Plantagenet).
1337-1453	Hundred Years' War between France and England.	Edward III (Plantagenet).
1431	Death of Joan of Arc.	Henry VI (Lancaster).
MODERN TIMES		
1515	Accession of François I (d 1547). (Renaissance architecture.)	Henry VIII (Tudor).
1562-98	Wars of Religion in France - destruction of many churches.	Elizabeth I (Tudor).
1589	Accession of Henri IV of France (d 1610). (Classical architecture 1589-1789.)	Elizabeth I.

Date	French history	Corresponding British history
1598	Edict of Nantes allowing Protestants freedom to worship.	Elizabeth I.
1610	Accession of Louis XIII (d 1643) (1622, king fights Protestants near St Gilles).	James I (Stuart).
1624-42	Richelieu prime minister. (1627-28 - siege of La Rochelle.)	Charles I (Stuart).
1643	Louis XIV - "the Sun King" (d 1715).	Charles I.
1685	Revocation of Edict of Nantes - 400,000 Huguenots (French Protestants) flee abroad, many to England.	James II (Stuart).
1774	Accession of Louis XVI.	George III (Hanover).
1789	French Revolution.	George III.
1792	First Republic (until 1804).	George III.
1793	Louis XVI guillotined 21 January.	George III.
1793-96	Wars of the Vendée.	George III.
1804	Napoleon I (Bonaparte) - First Empire (until 1814 when Napoleon is exiled to Elba.) *(Delicate, Classical-style architecture and furniture.)*	George III.
1814	Louis XVIII - First Restoration (until 1815).	George III.
1815	Napoleon returns for 100 days (Apr-June), later banished to St Helena. Louis de La Rochejaquelein attempts royalist invasion against the emperor. Louis XVIII - Second Restoration (d 1824).	George III.
1824	Charles X (exiled 1830).	George IV (Hanover).
1830	Louis-Philippe I (abdicates 1848 in favour of his grandson, the Comte de Paris).	William IV (Hanover).
1832	The Duchesse de Berry, daughter-in-law of Charles X, attempts a rebellion in the Vendée to place her son on the throne.	William IV.
1848	Second Republic (to 1852).	Victoria (Hanover).
1852	Napoleon III (Louis-Napoleon) - Second Empire (until 1870). *(Opulent architecture with wrought-iron features ; heavy, Victorian-style furniture.)*	Victoria.
1870	Third Republic (until 1940).	Victoria.
1940-44	Occupation of France (including Vendée) by Germany.	George VI (Windsor).

GENERAL HISTORY RELEVANT TO THE VENDÉE

The region was inhabited from prehistoric times - evidence in the shape of menhirs and dolmens dating from 2500BC and earlier is scattered all around, particularly in the Avrillé and Le Bernard areas in the south.

From the end of the 10th century, after the collapse of Charlemagne's empire, feudal castles began to appear in the Vendée at sites such as St-Mesmin, Ardelay, Noir-moutier, Tiffauges and Talmont.

From the 11th century AD much of France, including the area now known as the Vendée, saw the passage of thousands of pilgrims making their way from northern countries towards the shrine of St James the elder at Santiago de Compostela in north-west Spain. During the next two centuries abbeys, churches, convents, almshouses and hospitals sprung up along the most popular routes throughout western France to welcome and protect the 500,000 people who made the long journey. Unfortunately these fine Romanesque buildings have, throughout the Vendée, received heavy damage during the succession of wars that followed.

The marriage, in 1152, of Eleanor of Aquitaine to Henri Plantagenêt, Duke of Normandy (who, two years later, became King Henry II of England) combined her dowry of western France with his existing lands in the north to bring half of France into English hands. Their son Richard the Lionheart - Richard I of England - liked the Bas-Poitou (as the Vendée was then known) and often stayed in the region, notably at Talmont, either for fighting or hunting. He provided funds for a number of buildings including the abbey of Lieu-Dieu at Jard.

More than a century later, after his accession to the throne of England in 1327, Edward III made a claim through his mother's line to the crown of France. The resulting Hundred Years' War betwen the two countries - sustained by Richard II, Henry IV and Henry V - made much of north and western France into a battle-ground until 1453 when the French succeeded in winning back everything but the town of Calais (which they retrieved only in 1558).

Since the Vendée held a considerable number of influential Protestants ("les Réfor-més") the 36-year Wars of Religion that broke out in 1562 between Catholics and Protestants raged fiercely throughout the region and had much the same effect on the Vendée's monasteries and other religious buildings, as had the Hundred Years' War a century earlier. Eventually Henri IV, who had been brought up a Protestant and converted to Catholicism on his accession, granted freedom of worship to the Protestants in 1598, through the Edict of Nantes, and the wars came to an end.

Cardinal Richelieu - one-time bishop of Luçon - who was chief minister to Louis XIII between 1624 and 1642, saw the need to unite the whole of France under one crown. To reduce the power of the provincial dukes and princes, he ordered the destruction of their strongholds, reducing the Vendean castles like La Garnache, Les Essarts, Apremont and many others to ruins.

THE REVOLUTION AND THE WARS OF THE VENDÉE

After the Storming of the Bastille in 1789 and the Declaration of the First Republic in 1792 the new régime in France was total. The nobility was abolished. Priests who refused to swear allegience to the Republican government (rather than to the king, who had been the previous head of the Church) were deported and replaced with "loyal" ones. The names of towns and villages were changed from any with religious overtones (St-Gilles-sur-Vie becoming Port-Fidèle, for example). Even years, months, weeks and days were altered, with Year 1 starting on 22 September 1793, the 12 months (composed of three 10-day weeks) being renamed "Vendémiaire, Frimaire, Brumaire..." etc, and the days themselves being re-baptised "Primidi, Duodi, Tridi, Quartidi ..." and so on.

After having endured the absolute power of the king, many of the urban middle-classes embraced the new philosophies and the idea of a world of greater justice that they believed lay ahead. The downtrodden labouring classes, too, welcomed the Declaration of the Rights of Man, and looked forward to the abolition of the taxes that they had to pay to the crown.

Yet new ideas permeated only slowly to the Vendée, more than 200 miles from Paris. In this rural region, then known as Bas-Poitou, there was less social inequality than elsewhere. The aristocrats were less rich, their tenant farmers less poor, and the priests more revered in a religion that mixed elements of local superstition with orthodox Catholicism.

The Vendean peasants were, however, appalled to find that the Revolution removed their king (Louis XVI was executed in January 1793), forced on them the unpopular new priests loyal to the changed order, and called for the payment to the Republican government of even higher taxes than had been due under the monarchy. Worse, the confiscated goods of the old Church and deported clergy were thought to be lining the pockets of the bourgeoisie who had engineered for themselves top administrative posts. Ignoring the newly sworn-in priests who had been assigned to their churches, the Vendeans continued to worship clandestinely, protected by armed look-outs, at open-air Masses said by rebellious, pre-Revolutionary clergy.

The culmination, the spark that ignited the three years of horrific civil warfare, was the Republican government's decision in February 1793 to raise a 300,000-strong army for the defence of France's borders against threatened invasion by neighbouring countries which were opposed to the overthrow of the French monarchy. The people of Bas-Poitou and neighbouring départements refused to submit to formal conscription so Republican soldiers were sent in to draw names at random. Riots ensued. In March the town of Machecoul saw the massacre of its Republican sympathisers ; other villages followed suit. But generally counted as the start of the wars was the mass refusal of conscription, on 11 March 1793, by the people of St-Florent-le-Vieil on the river Loire, midway between Nantes and Angers, in the département of Maine-et-Loire. The populace routed the "Bleus" ("Blues", or Republican troops, sometimes referred to as "patriots"), and captured their cannon. (Nicknamed "Marie-Jeanne", this gun became a sort of talisman for the Grande Armée Catholique et Royale - as the Vendeans styled themselves - who used it in many battles.) The villagers of St-Florent called upon a humble carter, Jacques Cathelineau, to lead them and the others who joined the cause. He and former gamekeeper Jean-Nicolas Stofflet were working-class generals ; for the rest the Vendean peasants prevailed on trusted members of the local aristocracy to take command - François Athanase Charette de la Contrie, Louis de Lescure, Henri de la Rochejaquelein, the Duc d'Elbée - whose names have passed into local folklore.

After some spectacular Vendean victories in the early days at Bressuire, Thouars, Fontenay-le-Comte and Saumur, and then at Angers in June 1793 the "Blancs" ("Whites" or royalist Vendeans, also sometimes referred to by their opponents as "brigands") seemed invincible. Part of their success was due to the fact that they would disperse to their homes or hide in the countryside immediately after a battle, leaving no "army" for the Blues to seek out and destroy. (This autonomy also proved a problem - troops would often act on impulse, without awaiting orders.)

However the initially ill-prepared Republicans were soon reinforced by General

Kléber's crack troops known as the "Mayençais" who had been fighting on the German front, and victory turned to defeat at Nantes (where Cathelineau was mortally wounded after four months as general. The Whites lost Cholet, where Lescure was severely wounded, and then, in search of hoped-for reinforcements from England (where many of the French nobility had fled), the Vendean army made a seemingly-impossible dash north across the river Loire. Before his death - also from wounds sustained at Cholet - the Marquis de Bonchamps earned his place in history by refusing to allow his Vendean forces to massacre their 4,000-5,000 Republican prisoners, and insisting they be turned free.

This exodus, known as the "Virée de Galerne" evokes a kind of Dunkirk spirit in the region. Harried by the Blues, on 18 October 1793 the Vendeans ferried between 60,000 and 100,000 men, women and children across the wide and treacherous river - the wounded de Lescure among them. Their aim was to capture a suitable port - St-Malo in Brittany or Granville on the west side of the Cherbourg peninsula - ready to receive the expected English aid. During the epic journey the hungry, cold Vendeans marched some 200km north where they were joined by Breton guerrillas known as "Chouans" and laid siege, unsuccessfully, to the port of Granville in November. After a fruitless wait for help from England (William Pitt did, incidentally, send forces in 1795 who were repulsed during an attempt to land at Quiberon in Brittany), the Vendeans set off back towards the Loire. At Le Mans, 10,000 of them were cut down at the hands of the heavily-armed Republicans in the town. Tens of thousands more died, either in combat or from sickness or hunger. In December 1793 a few thousand managed to re-cross the Loire ; many others who were prevented from doing the same fled west where 6,000 fell victim to Republican troops in the forest of Savenay west of Nantes ; the few who escaped hid in impenetrable countryside or in the marshland around Guérande.
Determined that such insurrection should never happen again, the Republican

neral Turreau gave orders that "colonnes infernales" ("fiery columns" of troops)
ould lay waste every village and kill every remaining person in the département of
s-Poitou - that would henceforth be renamed "Vendée". From early 1794 these
ces passed from village to village burning, pillaging and massacring. At Les Lucs-
r-Boulogne 563 people - women, children and old men - were shot as they knelt in
urch to pray for delivrance (the tale is told today in the stained-glass windows of
e village's more recent church). At Les Sables-d'Olonne, blood from the guillotine
n thickly on to the town's golden sands ; at Nantes even the 1 $\frac{1}{2}$ minutes required
r this method of execution proved too slow and General Carrier, in charge of the
y, instituted a more efficient method by drowning whole boatloads of prisoners in
e river Loire.

ne few surviving Vendeans returned home to ruined houses, murdered families, and
reign of terror everywhere. They hid out among the gorse and bracken and the
rests of the bocage and continued to wage a guerrilla warfare for many months.
harette and Stofflet signed peace treaties with the Republicans in 1795, though
harette continued to lead skirmishes and ambushes against the Blues until his
pture at La Chabotterie in February 1796 and subsequent execution. (Stofflet had
en taken, and shot, a few weeks earlier.)

nder a treaty drawn up by the Republican General Hoche in 1799, freedom of
orship returned to France. Napoleon Bonaparte made supervision of the unruly
gion less difficult by transferring the capital from Fontenay-le-Comte to La Roche-
r-Yon in the geographical heart of the Vendée, and creating a new town of straight,
oad avenues to allow rapid deployment of his troops in any direction to quell future
risings.

lthough, with Charette's death, the wars had reached an end, some further attempts
ere made to rekindle them. During Napoleon's brief return to power in 1815, Louis
 La Rochejaquelein (brother of Henri) carried out an unsuccessful invasion near
roix-de-Vie. Seventeen years later the Duchesse de Berry tried to seize the French
rone for her son, the Duke of Bordeaux - grandson of Charles X.

ebate still rages as to whether the uprising that cost so many lives was truly
ontaneous or was engineered by landowners and priests reluctant to lose their
wer and fortunes. Atrocities were, no doubt, perpetrated by both Vendean and
epublican forces but, in the area where the memories live on, a certain amount of
as in the retelling of the stories is inevitable.

urist offices stock maps describing Les Routes de la Vendée Militaire. Among the
ost interesting sites and museums are :

a *Chabotterie*, manor house where Charette was captured and interrogated. Now an
formative museum and discovery centre.

es *Lucs-sur-Boulogne*, scene of a terrible massacre where 563 women, children
nd old people were locked in a church, shot and then burnt by Republicans.
lemorial chapel of Les Petits-Lucs, built on the site, and new, state-of-the-art
hemin de la Mémoire building ; stained-glass windows in village church.

loirmoutier Castle, for the bullet-ridden chair where d'Elbée was shot on the square
utside, also the painting of this scene, and other souvenirs.

e *Mont des Alouettes*, three remaining windmills of the seven whose sails were
sed to pass coded messages to the guerrilla warriors indicating the whereabouts of
ie Republican troops.

Museum of Puy-du-Fou, near Les Épesses.

Forest of Grasla, north of La Roche-sur-Yon, where 2,500 Vendeans hid out for six months in 1794.

Musée d'Art et d'Histoire, at Cholet, for paintings, objects and explanations in an ultra-modern setting.

Musée des Guerres de Vendée, at Les Sables-d'Olonne, for waxworks and documents.

Le Panthéon de la Vendée, cemetery at La Gaubretière where many combattants are buried.

For further reading :

In English :

"La Vendée" by Anthony Trollope. Historical novel, based closely on the memoirs of Madame de La Rochejaquelein, that first appeared in 1850. It paints a vivid picture of the early part of the war and of some of its principal characters. (Penguin, 1993)

"Citizens" by Simon Schama. Highly readable history of the French Revolution, with a substantial section on the Wars of the Vendée. (Viking, 1989)

In French :

"Blancs et Bleus dans la Vendée déchirée" by Jean-Clément Martin. Pocket-sized but information-packed book, alive with evocative paintings and drawings. (Découvertes Gallimard, 1987)

"Plein ciel sur les châteaux de Vendée" by Joseph Rouillé. Coffee-table volume of aerial views and descriptions of 76 Vendean castles and their fates during the wars. (Editions du Vieux Chouan, 1989)

"Je visite la Vendée" by Philippe Gaury. Useful, paperback visitors' guide to the region, with brief notes for each village on the events of the war. (Editions Hécate, 1993)

"Vendée Militaire 1793-1993" by Claude Jacquemart. Magazine-format, beautifully illustrated with paintings, engravings and present-day photographs of the Vendée, Maine-et-Loire and Deux-Sèvres. (Regard Régional, JFJ Publications, March 1993)

"L'Accent de ma mère" by Michel Ragon. Autobiography of a present-day writer and critic whose memories of his Vendean childhood are interwoven with accounts of the wars 150 years earlier. (Livre de Poche, Albin Michel, 1980)

"Les Mouchoirs rouges de Cholet" by Michel Ragon. Historical novel about the wars by the same author. (Livre de Poche, Albin Michel, 1984)

RECENT TIMES

Vast areas of pine and "chêne vert" (holm oak) were planted from the mid-19th century to anchor the shifting sands along the coast around St-Jean-de-Monts and north of Les Sables-d'Olonne. The coming of the railways in the 1860s helped to develop tourism around the ports of St Gilles-Croix-de-Vie and Les Sables d'Olonne where you can still see some fine examples of Victorian-period seaside architecture. The railways also provided a means of escape for many of the inhabitants of marshland farms, leading to a rural exodus around the turn of the century as the younger people found more lucrative work in urban areas. From the late 18th until the mid-20th century there was a coal-mining industry at Faymoreau-les-Mines, north-east of Fontenay-le-Comte.

For more than four years of the Second World War the Vendée was occupied by

German forces, who commandeered the coastline and denied access to many villages along it.

The wealth of the département today is based on agriculture (beef and dairy cattle, pigs and poultry in the woods and hills of the bocage, cereal-growing in the plain, sheep and cattle in the marshes, and early vegetables on the island of Noirmoutier), fishing (sardines, tuna, sole and langoustines, oysters and mussels), manufacture of clothes and shoes, boat-building (St-Gilles-Croix-de-Vie is the home of the world-famous Bénéteau yacht company), food-canning and the construction of agricultural machinery.

FAMOUS AND INFAMOUS VENDEANS

Memorable names connected with the Vendée include that of *Gilles de Rais* (1404-40), companion-in-arms of Joan of Arc and notorious in legend as the infamous "Bluebeard" ; *François Rabelais*, Renaissance humorist, writer, monk, and father of good living spent time at Fontenay-le-Comte and at Maillezais ; the inventor of modern algebra, *François Viète* (1540-1603) who was born at Fontenay-le-Comte, the département's capital in pre-Revolutionary times ; *Cardinal Richelieu* (1585-1642), prime minister to Louis XIII and bishop of Luçon from 1606 to 1622 ; *Nau l'Olonnois* (c1630-71), the bloodthirsty pirate from Olonne-sur-Mer who was chopped up and eaten by cannibals ; the statesman *Georges Clemenceau* (1841-1929) who drew up the Treaty of Versailles after the First World War, born near Mouilleron-en-Pareds and buried not far from Mouchamps ; the artist *Benjamin Rabier* (1864-1939) of La Roche-sur-Yon, creator of the cheery logo for Vache-qui-Rit (Laughing Cow) cheese ; distinguished soldier *Jean de Lattre de Tassigny* (1889-1952), born and buried at Mouilleron-en-Pareds ; and a present-day hero, yachtsman *Philippe Jeantot* of Les Sables-d'Olonne, who has masterminded the Vendée-Globe Challenge round-the-world, non-stop, single-handed sailing race.

PART II

CHAPTER 1

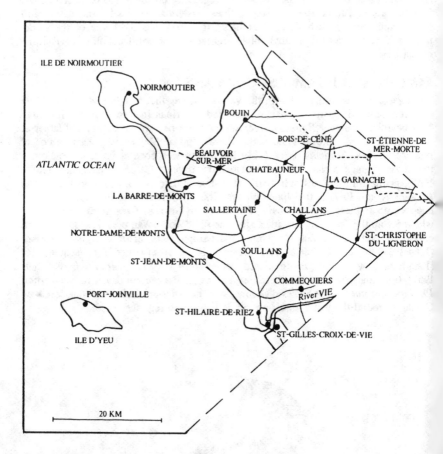

ILE DE NOIRMOUTIER

NOIRMOUTIER

BOUIN

BOIS-DE-CÉNÉ

ST-ÉTIENNE-DE-MER-MORTE

BEAUVOIR-SUR-MER

ATLANTIC OCEAN

CHATEAUNEUF

LA GARNACHE

LA BARRE-DE-MONTS

SALLERTAINE

CHALLANS

NOTRE-DAME-DE-MONTS

ST-CHRISTOPHE-DU-LIGNERON

SOULLANS

ST-JEAN-DE-MONTS

COMMEQUIERS

PORT-JOINVILLE

River VIE

ST-HILAIRE-DE-RIEZ

ILE D'YEU

ST-GILLES-CROIX-DE-VIE

20 KM

LA BARRE-DE-MONTS

Close to the coast, this village lies on the mainland side of the Noirmoutier bridg‹
about 16km north-west of Challans. From nearby Fromentine you can take a boat t
the island of Yeu (see page 42), 25km away (around 135F for a return trip). Fores
walks wind through the perfumed pine woods that hold the shifting sands in place.
Market : Saturday.

Ferme Marine de la Grande Prise. Monsieur von Unruh, the tall German owne‹
strides about a series of windswept, rectangular ponds giving a fascinating explan‹
tion (in English, if requested) of how he "plants" oysters and clams. Lying on th‹
mud in large, mesh pouches, they fatten peacefully over several years until they reac
a suitable size for restaurant tables. * 1 July-31 Aug, Fri 10am-noon. On th‹
Fromentine road, opposite Intermarché (tel : 51 49 38 70). 10F

Centre de Découverte du Marais Breton Vendéen. You need a good two hours to enjoy this open-air farming museum, 2km east of the main village. Since it is spread over 12 hectares, a fair amount of walking is required to appreciate the methods of fenland agriculture demonstrated in the context of a late-19th-century farm. You can peer into the simple reed-thatched "bourrines" (cottages) and earth-and-straw-walled outbuildings full of poultry, spotted pigs and turn-of-the-century farm machinery and read the interesting description of the region's salt industry alongside working salt-pans.

In summer there are frequent displays of traditional local activities like folk-dancing, and afternoons of boating (in flat-bottomed, punt-like craft known as "yoles"), dyke-jumping using punting poles ("saut à la ningle") or ploughing with sturdy Breton draught horses and elegantly-horned oxen. ♯ 16 Mar-11 Nov, Tues-Sat 10am-noon & 2-6pm, Sun 2-6pm (1-30 June, Tues-Sat 10am-noon & 2-6pm, Sun 3-7pm ; 1 July-31 Aug, daily 10am-7pm, Sun 3-7pm). Le Daviaud (tel : 51 68 57 03). 18F, children under 10 free.

BEAUVOIR-SUR-MER

Despite its name, this appealing little town 16km north-west of Challans is no longer on the coast but stranded 3km inland. Large signs on the west side give times of low tide when you can safely enjoy the unforgettable experience of driving your car across the Passage du Gois - the causeway 5km beyond the town that links the mainland with the island of Noirmoutier (see page 35).

Take a moment to visit the 12th- to 14th-century church of St Philbert - indeed, if you come from Challans by car, the D948 practically thrusts you in through the north door on a tight double bend.

Market : Thursday and Sunday.

Festival : Foire aux Moules (mussel festival), early August.

Race : Les Foulées du Gois (spectacular running race, with 1,500 competitors trying to beat the incoming tide across the 5.5km causeway), mid-June.

Chapel of Bourdevert. At a country crossroads on the D59, 4km east of the town, stands this enchanting, tiny church, dating from the 12th or 13th century and said to have been built by two sailors in gratitude for surviving a shipwreck in the days when the sea lapped against this spot. Push open the gnarled wooden door (the key may be obtained from a nearby address if locked) and step inside, where light streams through two simple arched windows on the side walls. A model ship is suspended from the painted rafters and, on either side of the ornate altar hang collections of babies' shoes - placed there by parents who come and pray to the Virgin to guide their children's first steps. Until quite recently a pilgrimage took place on the Feast of the Nativity ; today Mass is said at 3pm on the second Sunday of the month. ■

Port du Bec. The collection of spindly wooden jetties that protrude from either side of the canal leading to the sea have earned this picturesque little fishing village, 5km north-west of the town, its nickname of "the Chinese port". Lobster-pots litter the quays, brightly-painted boats lie alongside with coloured flags fluttering. High tide provides a scene of great activity as fishermen return from collecting their precious harvest of shellfish from the sea-bed "farms" in the bay of Bourgneuf. At the end of the harbour, parallel to the vast dyke that holds back the sea from the neighbouring marshes, is a road lined for 4km with oyster-producing enterprises. ■

Specialities : Oysters, clams, mussels.

BOIS-DE-CÉNÉ

Attractive village, 10km north of Challans, with a restored 14th-century chur standing in a leafy churchyard, and a few ancient houses that date from Renaissan times.

L'Abbaye de l'Ile Chauvet. Glance at a large-scale map and you can see that the s of this ancient abbey, just to the west of the village, was indeed once a small islar To reach it, you have to backtrack towards Châteauneuf and then turn right across t marshes (created by 12th-century monks who became prosperous from the resulti salt trade). A track leads through woods to a 19th-century mansion, behind which the romantic ruins of the church, founded by Benedictines in 1130, much damag by the English in 1381, and finally abandoned after its destruction by the Republica after the French Revolution. The guided tour leads through a handsome Romanesq doorway to the roofless chancel ; part of the refectory building still stands and y can see, in the former dormitory on the first floor, models of the surrounding lar scape in earlier times. * 1 July-8 Sept, Mon-Sun 2-6pm. Ile Chauvet (tel : 51 68 13 1' 15F, children 5F.

PINTA : la route du sel (Pistes Nouvelles et Traces Anciennes). This organisati offers some entrancing ways to discover the wide open spaces of the marshes usi the ancient salt routes. You can rent canoes by the hour from about 50F, or ta guided canoe, cycle or walking trips, from the well-signposted PINTA farm in t heart of the Ile Chauvet marshland. Wildlife includes herons, buzzards, malla lapwings, and even storks nesting precariously on the treetops. It can be scorching a hot summer day ; early-morning or late-afternoon bookings are recommend during heatwaves. ♯ Ile Chauvet (tel : 51 49 22 17). Details and booking via most loc tourist offices, or direct through PINTA, Place de la Vieille Eglise, Sallertaine (tel : 93 03 40), or 33 Rue de Nantes, Challans (tel : 51 68 27 84).

BOUIN

This large village (once an island), 20km north-west of Challans, is the most impe tant oyster centre of the region. Old houses and narrow lanes surround a chur where, in July and August, you can take a guided tour up the tower for a panoram view across the oyster beds, the bay of Bourgneuf, and the 14km of dykes th protect the village from invasion by the sea (it has, in fact, been submerged by t waters at least 30 times - the last in 1940). The oyster fishermen work on the coast the nearby Port du Bec (see page 31), Port des Champs and Port des Brochets.

Market : Saturday.

Festival : Les Gobeurs d'Huîtres (oyster-eating festival), early August.

Port la Roche. Picturesque hamlet at the junction of the river Falleron and the ma "étier" (canal), off the D59, midway between Bouin and Machecoul. Its three loc that control the water levels make it the hydraulic hub of the surrounding marshlan the tranquil Marais de Machecoul. An exploration of the surrounding lanes leads y through unforgettably beautiful scenery beneath wide skies, where the narrow cana are lined with reeds taller than the single-storey houses and the fields are st enclosed by traditional slip-rails instead of gates. PINTA (Pistes Nouvelles et Trac Anciennes) offers day-long canoe trips (with barbecue lunch) through the car network of these former salt-marshes. Details and booking via most local tour offices, or direct through PINTA, Place de la Vieille Eglise, Sallertaine (tel : 51 93 40), or 33 Rue de Nantes, Challans (tel : 51 68 27 84).

CHALLANS

As the "capital of the duck" Challans, 16km from the coast, is to France what Aylesbury is to England. These birds used to be reared in enormous numbers in the surrounding marshes, though they are now giving way somewhat to free-range black chickens (you'll pass many fields where these birds are scratching around outside large, modern barns). Though the ravages of the Vendée wars (see page 24) have not left much of historical merit, this is a charming market town, bristling with restaurants and smart shops - look for the pedestrianised Rue Gobin, and try home-made chocolates and pâtisseries from Litou in Rue Carnot or Billet on Place Aristide Briand (alongside the market-hall).

However, Challans is renowned, above all, for its terrific market-day on Tuesdays, when people come from all around to snap up the fresh fish, vegetables, cheese (particularly delicious goat's cheeses from a farm at nearby La Garnache) and other produce in the covered "halles" (market-hall) and to look over the hundreds of stalls selling clothes, farm equipment, gadgets for the home and even live poultry that fill the streets and squares with local colour.

Market : Tuesday (throughout the town), Friday (covered food-hall only).

Specialities : Duck of Challans (often cooked in Muscadet), free-range black chicken of Challans, black-domed "tourteau au fromage" (a sort of cheesecake), "flan maraîchin" (pastry cases, filled with egg custard).

Brocante : Toutoccas, about 3km from Challans on the D948 La Roche-sur-Yon road. Tues-Sat 9.30am-12.30pm & 2.30-7pm, Sun 3-7pm.

Autrefois Challans... la foire. On four Thursdays in July and August each year the clock is turned back and more than 1,000 people dress up in turn-of-the-century costume. Looking, no doubt, the image of their own grandparents, the men sport blue denim smocks and heavy clogs or the traditional marshland garb of black close-fitting trousers and short, matador-style jacket, with jaunty, black, small-brimmed hats. The women often wear the face-shading white bonnet known as a "quichenotte" (supposedly a corruption of the English "Kiss not" from the time of English occupation during the Hundred Years' War) that were a common sight among farmers' wives and market clients until about 15 years ago. Horse-drawn carts wend their way through the streets, farmers trade ducks and chickens, children re-enact schoolroom scenes or old-style sporting events ; the old folk are busy spinning, weaving and playing local games like "l'aluette" (a picturesque card game) or "palets" (a noisy contest involving lumps of metal thrown at a board). Dozens of crafts old and new are demonstrated alongside the post office. You can sample the local ham and "mogettes" (white haricot beans), or tuck into barbecued sardines and local wines at long tables in the streets. * Two Thursdays in July and two Thursdays in August, 10am-7pm. Free.

Musée d'Oiseaux et de Mammifères. Museum 3km south-west of Challans, displaying hundreds of stuffed animals and birds in re-creations of seaside, lake and forest settings, plus collections of shells and of bird's eggs. Outside is a garden filled with 350 different fuchsias. * 1 July-31 Aug, daily 2-7pm. La Morinière, Route de St-Jean-de-Monts (tel : 51 68 24 12). 10F.

CHATEAUNEUF

Small village 8km north of Challans. The parish church contains one of the oldest bells in the Vendée, dating from 1487.

Le Petit Moulin. The sails of this windmill, built in 1703 still provide the power to grind corn, though now purely for animal feed. Monsieur Vrignaud, third-generation miller, explains the process animatedly (ask for an English information sheet to help you keep up) as he demonstrates the engaging of the wooden gears and adjusting of the slatted sails. The mighty oak shaft that carries the sail mechanism is changed every 50 years, the latest one having been installed in 1994. Keep an eye on children among the clanking machinery and on the spiral stairs, which are fairly perilous even for a nimble adult. ♯ 1 Apr-30 Sept, Sun & public holidays 2-7pm (1 June-30 Sept, daily 2-7pm). Signposted from village centre (tel : 51 49 31 07). 10F, children 5F.

Au Panier de Châteauneuf. Farm shop near the windmill, selling all sorts of local poultry, eggs, preserves, jams, wine, honey and the widely-enjoyed mogettes. 4 Rue du Moulin (tel : 51 49 44 87). ■ Fri 3-7pm (1 June-30 Sept, daily 3-7pm ; 1 July-31 Aug, daily 10am-noon & 3-7pm).

COMMEQUIERS

Village on the edge of the bocage, 9km south-east of Challans, that was a centre of considerable feudal power until the end of the Middle Ages.

Market : Wednesday.

Festivals : Bourse aux Armes (sale of old firearms and related equipment), early August.

Château. Accessible by a track leading off the D754 north of the village, these imposing ruins belong to a 15th-century moated castle that was demolished on orders from Cardinal Richelieu in 1628. The eight handsome, round towers, once excellent look-out points over the marshes beyond, give the building the appearance of the best kind of sandcastle. Take a wooden footbridge across the water-filled moat to explore the inner secrets. ■

Dolmen de Pierres-Folles. Take a left turning about 1km south-west of the village, off the D754 St-Gilles road, then go left again and stop on the edge of a copse. After following a small footpath through the undergrowth for a few metres you come to a huge dolmen - two-thirds collapsed - all the more mysterious and impressive for being buried in this out-of-the-way spot. One of its stones is said to bear the footprint of the Virgin. ■

LA GARNACHE

Large village 6km north-east of Challans, dominated by the ruins of its feudal castle.

Market : Thursday.

Specialities : "Le Garnachoix", a goat's cheese.

Crafts : Wooden-toymaking, by Jean and Jacqueline Curtenaz at Varnes (signposted off the Nantes road).

Château Féodal. Ruins of the 13th- to 15th-century stronghold built by the lords of La Garnache, partially destroyed in 1622 at the behest of Louis XIII, and further still under the Revolution. You can stroll around some of the ramparts and look at the remains of the defences ; elegant gardens have been planted in the former moat by the present owners who are slowly uncovering more of the crumbling stonework from beneath the stranglehold of ivy. A room in the 12th-century keep contains displays of models in medieval costume. Explanatory panels with notes in English and French. * Early July-mid-September, daily 2.30-7pm. Route de Nantes (tel : 51 4 12 65). 15F, children 8F.

Musée Passé et Traditions. In a small, turn-of-the-century farmworker's cottage is a comprehensive and well-explained collection of farm implements, local costume, customs and furniture. ♯ 1 June-30 Sept ; Sat, Sun 2.30-7pm (15 June-15 Sept, daily 2.30-7pm). La Borderie, Route de St Christophe. 12F, children free.

ILE DE NOIRMOUTIER

Barely 1km off the coast, this long, thin island 20km north-west of Challans is connected to the mainland by a toll bridge from Fromentine and, at low tide, by "Le Gois", a 5.5km causeway which is one of the wonders of France. Thanks to a microclimate, Noirmoutier produces the first yellow pompoms of mimosa in the dark depths of February, delectable early potatoes served at the smartest tables in France, and a tremendous harvest of fish - particularly conger eel, sole and squid. The island's economy once depended to a great extent on the production of salt, and you can still see the rectangular drying-pans (especially just north of the road from Noirmoutier-en-l'Ile to L'Épine) where seawater is allowed to evaporate, leaving crystals to be raked up into little white pyramids. A blue-signposted "Route de l'Ile" leads motorists and cyclists around the lanes and through villages of low, whitewashed houses to some of the island's prettiest spots.

The colourful, animated port of L'Herbaudière is a centre for fishing and pleasure craft on the north coast of the island. At Bois-de-la-Chaize, a wooded area on the north-east coast, the air in February is heavy with the perfume of mimosa ; the sheltered beach - distinctly Breton in atmosphere - is so popular in high summer that parking is impossible (better to go by bike or on foot). La Guérinière, on the south coast, is an attractive village, strung out along the old main road of the island (now by-passed by the super-highway that connects the bridge with the island's capital) which is lined with shops selling beach-balls, shrimping nets and other Monsieur-Hulot-type holiday equipment ; the late film director Jacques Démy (who made "Les Parapluies de Cherbourg") owned one of the nearby windmills as a holiday home.

The island's capital is Noirmoutier-en-l'Ile, a trim, pretty place with smart shops and restaurants surrounding the impressive 12th-century castle, but almost impossible to get to by car on summer afternoons. At low tide the causeway lures hundreds of extra vehicles on to the fast dual-carriageway that rockets them towards the little town, and then leaves them stuck fast on the outskirts.

Markets : Monday at L'Herbaudière ; Tuesday, Friday and Sunday at Noirmoutier-en-l'Ile ; Thursday and Sunday at La Guérinière.

Festivals : Festival de la Peinture (art festival), early July ; Foire aux Antiquaires (two-day antiques fair), mid-July and mid-August ; Foire à la Brocante (flea market), mid-July and mid-August ; Craft markets, mid-July to late August.

Specialities : Salt production, early mimosa and potatoes, fish, the marshland plant "salicorne" (samphire), butter with Noirmoutier salt.

Le Gois. On no account miss a drive, either to or from the island, along this submersible roadway that was the only access until 1971. Be sure to return for a look at high tide as well - you can see why a few unwary folk each year need to climb the sturdy wooden refuges known as "balises" to await rescue by boat ! The ultimate romantic experience is to cross it on a moonlit night. Ask for tide-tables ("horaires des marées") at any tourist office nearby and look at the column marked "passage du Gois" - the route is practicable for about an hour and a half either side of low tide (times are also shown on huge roadside notices at Beauvoir-sur-Mer and on the Noirmoutier side of the causeway). Do not risk crossing outside the recommended times - the water swirls back across the road at astonishing speed. Locals take advantage of extra-low tides to park their cars on the mud and scrabble far afield for cockles and other shellfish. The handsome bridge that now provides alternative - if more prosaic - access costs 8F each way by car. For the return to the mainland, follow signposts to the quaintly-termed "continent" - either "par pont à péage" (by toll bridge) or "par Le Gois" (by causeway). ■

Château of Noirmoutier-en-l'Ile. Imposing, dry-moated castle in the centre of the island's capital, visible from far across the salt marshes. During its turbulent, 800-year history the building served as a prison for insurgents of the Paris Commune in 1871, as a centre for internees in the First World War, a victualling centre for the Germans during the Occupation, and then held German prisoners after the Liberation. Steep stone steps lead to rooms displaying stuffed birds, navigational equipment, maritime maps, archaeological remains and local history - anyone of gory disposition will appreciate the bullet-ridden chair in which the Vendéen general the Duc d'Elbée was shot, in January 1794, by Republican troops in the elegant square outside the castle gates. On the top floor is a proudly-displayed but rather gaudy collection of lustre-ware from Jersey, the type of souvenir cherished by 18th- and 19th-century sailors and fishermen. ♯ 1 Feb-15 Nov, Wed-Mon 10am-noon & 2.30-5.30pm (1 July-31 Aug, daily 10am-7pm). Place d'Armes (tel : 51 39 10 42). 20F, children 10F.

Église St-Philbert. Beneath the church which lies to the north of the castle, accessible from near the side of the main altar, is a beautiful 11th-century crypt that holds the empty tomb of St Philbert, founder of a monastery on the island in AD674. (The saint's remains were removed 162 years later to St Philbert-de-Grand-Lieu (see page 105), and later to Tournus in Burgundy.) Press the button for a taped explanation of the church's history, with musical accompaniment. ■

Sealand. All the names on the fishmonger's slab come to life in the huge tanks that line the walls of this excellent aquarium : turbots swim with elegant wave-like movements of their bodies, langoustes and crabs stalk haughtily across the gravel floor, small sharks cruise thoughtfully through the water, octopuses pulsate in the depths, and the sinister "murène" (a kind of extra-ferocious eel) lurks in rocky crevices. Sealions splash in a semi-open-air pool - you can go down steps to watch their underwater antics from behind 60mm-thick glass. A rather poor video purports to tell you about the sea life, but concentrates mostly on telling you how good the different species are to eat. Some jewel-coloured tropical fish are on view, with interesting explanations for anyone who is thinking of keeping them at home. ■ Daily 10am-12.30pm & 2-7pm (1 July-31 Aug, 10am-midnight). Le Vieux Port, Noirmoutier-en-l'Ile (tel : 51 39 08 11). 38F, children 25F.

Naval Construction Museum. The different stages in the building of wooden boats are explained in a reconstructed 19th-century workshop, where the graceful curves of the ships' timbers complement those of the solid rafters of the roof above. Also on show - appropriately, since this quayside building is an old "salorge" or salt warehouse - is information on the island's salt industry that made the fortune of the medieval monks who set it up ; tours of the salt beds can be arranged. ♯ 1 Apr-15 Nov, Tues-Sun 10am-noon & 2.30-6pm (1 July-31 Aug, daily 10am-7pm). Rue de l'Écluse, Noirmoutier-en-l'Ile (tel : 51 39 24 00). 15F, children 7F.

(Continue along the track beyond the museum for a melancholy sight - a nautical "graveyard" containing the skeletons and hulks of boats of all types and in various stages of disintegration.)

Musée des Arts et Traditions Populaires. The islanders' traditions, activities and way of life linked to fishing, salt production, farming and the manufacture of linen at the turn of the century. Collections of tools are on display, and a series of rooms shows typical interiors of island homes. ⇥ 1 Feb-15 Nov, Tues-Sun 2.30-5pm (15 June-15 Sept, daily 10am-noon & 2.30-6.30pm). Place de l'Église, La Guérinière (tel : 51 39 41 39). 15F, children 7F.

NOTRE-DAME-DE-MONTS

Seaside village 6km south of the Noirmoutier toll bridge and just north of the huge resort of St-Jean-de-Monts, Notre-Dame has the finest-textured sand on the Vendée coast. The vast beach is ideal for sand-yachting and for the village's annual international frisbee tournament.
Market : Sunday.

Château d'Eau. Choose a clear day to take the lift up the 70m water tower, 3km east of the village on the D82, for a bird's eye view of the marshes, the coast, the Ile d'Yeu and the island of Noirmoutier. Pack a map and binoculars if you've got them. ⇥ June 1-Sept 15, Tues-Sun 10.30am-12.30pm & 3-7pm. La Croix, Notre-Dame-de-Monts (tel : 51 58 86 09). 7F50.

ST-CHRISTOPHE-DU-LIGNERON

The restored 17th-century castle (now offering bed-&-breakfast), on the edge of the village, is a landmark for motorists 9km south-east of Challans on the D178 road towards La Roche-sur-Yon. The village is now famous among brocante-hunters for its two enormous summer flea markets.
Festivals : Fête des Battages (old-time harvest), late July.

Les Puces Ligneronnaises. Vast open-air flea market held twice a year on the sports ground at the northern end of the village. Stalls, spread over two or three fields, offer many happy hours of treasure-hunting among chests of huge, monogrammed linen sheets, racks of old picture-postcards, and furniture, glass and bric-à-brac of all kinds. * Mid-July & mid-Aug, Sun 10am-5pm. 1F (for charity).

ST-ÉTIENNE-DE-MER-MORTE (Loire-Atlantique)

Picturesque village perched on the side of a hill above the Falleron river, 13km north-east of Challans. As well as its 19th-century church, there is a pretty, free-standing bell-tower with a pointed spire - the remains of a much earlier church into which the infamous Gilles de Rais (see Tiffauges, page 94) stormed on Whit Sunday 1440, at the head of a band of men. In the middle of High Mass, he seized Jean le Ferron, one of the congregation, and dragged him to his nearby castle at Machecoul. For this act of sacrilege, he was later arrested and taken to Nantes, where he confessed to his many horrible crimes before being hanged on 26 October 1440.
Specialities : Snails, Gros-Plant wines.

Ferme aux Escargots. The enterprising Jean-Gilles Thomas offers guided tours tof his thriving snail farm (signposted off the D13 between Paulx and Touvois). The young, produced in February, are fattened until September in large concrete pens. If you can't quite face preparing them yourself, you can buy ready-made products on the spot in the form of snail pâté or tiny, snail-filled vol-au-vents. ⇥ 1 May-15 Sept, Mon-Sat, 3-7pm. 7 La Chevalerie (tel : 40 31 10 49). 15F.

ST-GILLES-CROIX-DE-VIE

Twin towns on either side of the estuary of the river Vie - with Croix-de-Vie to the north. Here, the railway line from Paris terminates at the buffers alongside both the fishing harbour and the main street. In the fish shop opposite you can admire the glistening produce and watch lobsters and langoustes pick their way carefully around an aquarium let into the wall. The port is renowned for sardines and anchovies, and for a large canning industry (trade name "Les Dieux") for these, and for other products like fish soup and tuna. (From April to September you can buy direct from the Gendreau company's shop at 76 Quai de la République, opposite the railway line on the north side of the river.)

The sea is the background to the towns' other claim to fame as the headquarters of the Bénéteau boatbuilding company that has become the largest volume yacht manufacturer in the world. Many of its products can be seen moored in the Croix-de-Vie marina.

You can take boats from here for the 65-min crossing to the Ile d'Yeu (Garcie Ferrande, tel : 51 55 45 42) ; and the 45-min Navijet (tel : 51 54 15 15). Half-day and whole-day cruises are also possible on a "vieux gréement", an old, sail-powered fishing boat (ask at the tourist office).

Across the river, at St Gilles-sur-Vie, is a vast stretch of beach. In high summer choose your time carefully here - it can be impossibly crowded at high water when the incoming tide compresses sunbathers onto an ever-narrower ribbon of sand. Some charming French domestic seaside architecture along the roads leading to the Grande Plage harks back to the mid-19th-century when the newly-created railway network made seaside holidays fashionable. An attractive old church (in the tower of which one of Napoleon's generals was killed in 1815, during the second Vendean uprising) stands on the little market square.

Markets : Tuesday, Thursday and Sunday, St-Gilles-sur-Vie ; Wednesday and Saturday, Croix-de-Vie.

Festivals : International jazz festival, Whitsuntide (May/June) ; Fête de la Mer (festival of the sea), mid July ; Festival des Vins de Loire (Loire wine festival), late July ; Fête du Port, early August ; Foire aux Oignons (two-day onion festival), late August.

Specialities : Sardines, fresh or canned.

Maison du Pêcheur. A low, whitewashed house in one of Croix-de-Vie's oldest streets, just across from the tourist office, furnished with items typical of a local fisherman's home in the 1920s. * 1 July-31 Aug, Wed-Mon 10.30am-12.30pm & 5-7pm. 22 Rue du Maroc, Croix-de-Vie. 5F

Noce maraîchine. Wedding feasts staged each week in a barn/restaurant 9km north-east of St-Gilles, with food, dancing and lively entertainment in the traditional style of the surrounding marshland communities. Book your place in advance ; you will share a table with other "guests", just like you would at the real thing. You need to be robust enough to cope with local dishes like calf's head and ox tongue, and be prepared to participate in the energetic dancing. ■ Fri 8.30pm-2am. 230F (includes wine). Le Pouct'on, Le Pas Opton, Le Fenouiller (tel : 51 54 00 42).

ST-HILAIRE-DE-RIEZ

Just over 5km north of St-Gilles-Croix-de-Vie, the village embraces the rocky resort of Sion-sur-l'Océan and the holiday village of Merlin-Plage as well as Notre-Dame-de-Riez, a little farther inland. The 17th-century church contains several religious paintings by Henry Simon (1910-87), one of the region's best-known artists.

Markets : Sunday, Notre-Dame de Riez (15 June-15 Sept) ; Monday morning and Wednesday and Saturday afternoons at Merlin-Plage (summer season only) ; Tuesday and Friday, Sion ; Thursday and Sunday, St Hilaire-de-Riez.

Brocante : Maison Macker, just north of the roundabout on the D38, north of St Hilaire (open every afternoon) ; Chez Pierrot, on the D83, south of Notre-Dame-de-Riez (closed Thursday).

Corniche Vendéenne. Just north of Croix-de-Vie, at Sion, the shoreline rises to provide the first cliffs of the Vendée. The area is crowded in summer, but provides a series of sheltered coves to protect out-of-season visitors, and dramatic effects of wind and water above, for those who brave the autumn gales.

Atlantic Toboggan. Family water-park, located 7km north-west of St-Hilaire, with five 15m water-chutes (only the bravest should embark on the "kamikaze") and huge pools, plus picnic-spots and playgrounds. ♯ Late May-mid-Sept, daily 10am-7pm. Les Becs, Merlin-Plage, on the D123 (tel : 51 58 05 37). 65F, children 55F, under-threes free.

Bourrine du Bois-Juquaud. Snappily-entitled "Unité Agro-Pastorale du Bois-Juquaud", this limewashed, earth-built cottage and its outbuildings 4km north of St-Hilaire, thatched with reeds in local style are the subjects of countless picture-postcards. Through its examples of traditional furniture, building materials and a typical vegetable garden, it gives a valuable insight into the self-sufficient life of the peasants in the surrounding marshland (some of whom still live in similar style today). ♯ 31 Mar-31 Oct, Tues-Sun 2-6pm (1 June-14 Sept, Tues-Sun 10am-noon & 2.30-6.30pm ; 1 July-31 Aug, daily 10am-noon & 2.30-6.30pm). Le Pissot (tel : 51 49 27 37). 8F, children under 11 free.

Memorial to Louis de la Rochejaquelein. A simple stone cross in a small cluster of trees at Les Mattes (sometimes written "Les Mathes"), 6km north-west of St-Hilaire off the D59, marks the place where the Vendean general fell, rallying his troops, on 4 June 1815. Brother of the Vendean leader Henri de la Rochejaquelein, he had landed from England a few days earlier and embarked on a short-lived attempt to revive the royalist cause and drive Napoleon's forces from the marshes. A thousand soldiers from each side faced one another on this sandy terrain, at that time the only way through the marshes from St-Gilles to Soullans. ■

ST-JEAN-DE-MONTS

Children adore pedalling four-seater "quadricycles" along the seafront of this large seaside resort, 17km west of Challans. The 7km beach and modern esplanade are, of course, the main attractions of the town ; however, the old fishing village, now half a mile inland, contains an attractively restored church with a 17th-century bell-tower, its pointed spire roofed with wooden tiles.

Markets : Wednesday and Saturday, near the church in the old village (daily in summer) ; daily, Rue du Marché (near the beach) during the summer.

Golf : Golf de St-Jean-de-Monts. Testing, 5,962-metre course, its first nine holes winding through pine trees, the second nine lying alongside the sea in Scottish-links style (see page 15 for details of Vendée Golf Pass). Avenue des Pays-de-Monts (tel : 51 8 82 73). ■

JNTA (Pistes Nouvelles et Traces Anciennes). Guided, magical, pre-dawn canoe ours through the misty wilderness of the marshes. As the sun rises you'll see and ear lapwings, buzzards, water rats and many other creatures. Best to wear layers of othing that you can peel off as the sun climbs higher. * July, 5.30am ; Aug 6am ;

return around 12.30pm. PINTA (tel : 51 58 00 48). Details and booking via most local tourist offices (or see Sallertaine, below). 190F including picnic breakfast.

SALLERTAINE

A delightful village on what was once an island, dominating the flat landscape of the Marais Breton 8km west of Challans. Formerly a bustling centre where farming families from the surrounding, isolated farms would congregate on Sundays by flat-bottomed boat to attend Mass, it now attracts artists and craftspeople and makes a highly enjoyable visit. For an unusual experience, take coffee at the Chêne Vert café. Its bar is decorated with bizarre items of taxidermy (a gigantic boar's head, a cat and mouse, a rat, the bust of a cockerel), the handiwork of the eccentric "patronne" (owner's wife), who has also planted up an attractive garden at the back enhanced by other creatures - some alive, some stuffed.

Exposition Maraîchine. Three-quarters of a wonderful 12th-century church, saved in the nick of time from total destruction in 1915 by René Bazin (the novelist whose 1899 novel "La Terre qui Meurt" will conjure up for French-readers an unforgettable picture of farming life in the marshes a century ago). The 18th-century "improvements" to the building have failed to erase its atmosphere, and behind the flaking whitewash you can just make out fragments of some ancient frescoes. Where once the congregation sat, are slightly incongruous tableaux showing costumed figures in typical scenes of marshland life. Unfortunately the poses of the retired shop-window dummies suggest, falsely, that the local peasantry was composed entirely of doe-eyed young men and skinny, over-made-up damsels, but the venue itself more than makes up for these shortcomings. * Late June-mid Sept, daily 2.30-7pm (1 Jul-31 Aug, daily 10.30am-12.30pm & 2.30-7pm). Vieille Église (tel : 51 35 51 95). 8F.

Craft shops. These vary each year, but include a maker of attractive wooden toys, art galleries, dried-flower products, local farm produce and preserves, painting on silk, and many novel decorative ideas. *

PINTA (Pistes Nouvelles et Traces Anciennes). One-hour guided canoe trips around the former island of Sallertaine make an excellent introduction to the Marais Breton : hourly throughout the day ; 50F, children free. A longer trip, starting at 5.30pm, enables you to view the marshland fauna as dusk falls and enjoy a convivial evening meal before returning through the dark, narrow canals at around 11.30pm ; 235F including dinner and wine. All-day mountain-bike excursions to the Ile Chauvet and back, via 25km of marshes, woodland trails and bridlepaths : July & August, Wed 9.30am-5pm ; 170F (includes bicycle hire). ‡‡ PINTA office, Place de la Vieille Église (tel : 51 93 03 40).

Le Moulin de Rairé. The miller takes visitors up rickety wooden staircases to visit three floors of his working windmill - built in 1560, 3km north-west of Sallertaine and claimed to be the only wind-powered one in France to have been in continuou use since its construction. If your French is rusty, it would be advisable to obtain one of the English leaflets to clarify Monsieur Burgaud's enthusiastic explanations and demonstrations ; anybody with small children in tow will need to watch out for th flailing machinery and narrow, open stairs. The view across the marshes from the top-floor window, regularly interrupted by the wood-slatted sails creaking past, i breathtaking. In a barn near by is an interesting display of photographs and milling equipment. ‡‡ 1 May-15 Sept, public holidays 2-6pm (15 June-15 Sept, daily 2-6pm 1 July-31 Aug, daily 10am-noon & 2-6.30pm). Off the D103 St-Urbain road (tel : 51 3 51 82). 12F, children 6F.

La Bourrine à Rosalie. About 5km west of Sallertaine nestles a reed-thatched, two-roomed cottage inhabited until recently by the doughty old lady whose photograph hangs on the wall. The simple, whitewashed interior gives an (albeit rather sanitised) image of life in one of these isolated farms, where beds needed long legs to stay above winter flood-waters that regularly rose to 20cm above the level of the earth floors. Neat labels explain the origins and purposes of items on display. Outside are a small canalside orchard, some ducks and a donkey. ⌗ 1 Apr-15 Sept, Sat, Sun & public holidays 3-7pm (15 June-15 Sept, daily 3-7pm ; 1 July-31 Aug, daily 10.30am-12.30pm & 2-7pm). On the C116, between Sallertaine and St-Jean-de-Monts (tel : 51 49 43 60/ 51 68 73 61). 7F, children 5F.

Festivals : Fête à la Bourrine à Rosalie (traditional dancing and demonstrations of country skills and crafts), 15 August.

SOULLANS

Large village on the frontier of the bocage and the marshes, 6km south of Challans.
Market : Friday.
Festivals : Foire à la Brocante (antique fair), April.
Crafts : Batteur de cuivre (copper-smith), 39 chemin de Massoté, Terres-Noires (3km north-east of Soullans, off the D32).

Musée Milcendeau-Jean Yole. Charming museum in the heart of the countryside about 3km south of Soullans, devoted to two of the village's most celebrated inhabitants - the painter Charles Milcendeau (1872-1919) and his contemporary, the doctor, then writer and politician, Léopold Robert (1878-1956) who, under the name of Jean Yole, published many books in praise of the Vendée.

In the first room of this low, whitewashed cottage that was once Milcendeau's home are a series of portraits showing the artist's neighbours as exactly the sort of ruddy-cheeked country folk you see in the markets today, and some dramatic, wintry views of the marshland scenes that surrounded him. (If you have driven across parched August pastures to reach the museum, you may feel that he went a bit over the top here, but February's rains can still produce the same effect today.) A good audio-visual presentation is given on the artist's life and travels in Spain, which influenced much of his other painting. The rest of the first building is taken up with photographs illustrating the life of Jean Yole (see also Vendrennes, page 95).

In the second house a real surprise awaits when you enter the painter's bedroom-cum-studio, for Milcendeau covered every inch of its whitewashed walls with Spanish/Arab-inspired frescoes in vivid blues and yellows, creating stylised birds, flowers and other designs. Stuffed pigeons on the windowsill add to the frozen-in-time atmosphere and the reshaping of the doorways accentuates the room's unexpectedly Moorish feel. ⌗ Mid Mar-11 Nov, Tues-Sat 10am-noon & 2-6pm, Sun 2-6pm (1 June-30 Sept, Tues-Sat 10am-noon & 2-6pm, Sun 3-7pm ; 1 July-31 Aug, Tues-Sat 10am-noon & 3-7pm, Sun 3-7pm). Le Bois Durand (tel : 51 35 03 84). 13F, children free.

Menhirs. A large standing-stone - the Menhir de la Palissonnière - can be seen in the middle of a field on the D82 Commequiers road, about 4km south-east of Soullans. Another - the Pierre-Levée - near the Gîte du Tourne-Pierre restaurant on the D69 Challans road, about 3km north of the village, is the subject of a legend saying that any young girl who causes it to move by climbing on it will be married within the year (it is reputed to shift slightly, if you put your foot on the right spot). ■

ILE D'YEU

Various ports on the mainland offer trips to Port-Joinville, the capital of this picturesque island of 23sq km that lies an hour's boat-ride off the coast (a bit less by hydrofoil) to the west of St-Gilles-Croix-de-Vie. However, at a minimum of around 130F return per adult (and more than 71F for a 4- to 12-year-old), it could be an expensive proposition for a family. You need to book ahead in the peak season, and it is a good idea to hire bicycles on arrival to explore the island - perfectly feasible in a day (it is not worth taking your own - the ferry companies charge around 65F to transport each one). A tandem is recommended only for couples with the most rock-solid of marriages.

There are not many cars on the gorse-lined lanes, and the island's houses seem to be bleached by the 4,500 hours of sun that beats down on them each year. Don't miss the pretty fishing harbour of Port-de-la-Meule, overlooked by the tiny, whitewashed chapel of Notre-Dame-de-Bonne-Nouvelle, and the ghostly ruins of the feudal medieval fortress (the Vieux Château), both on the rocky south coast.

The north side of the island is full of inviting, sandy coves. Among neolithic monuments is the enormous "pierre tremblante" near Port-de-la-Meule that will move if pressed in a particular place, and a large dolmen in the western corner of the island. The village of St-Sauveur, in the centre, has an attractive Romanesque church. In 1945 the 90-year-old Marshal Pétain was incarcerated in the gloomy, impregnable Pierre-Levée fort after his death sentence for treason (for having headed the Vichy government during the Second World War) was commuted to life imprisonment. He died six years later, and is buried in the island's cemetery.

Boats from Fromentine and St-Gilles-Croix-de-Vie take around 65min (from St Jean-de-Monts 45min) ; Navijet from La Fosse (on Noirmoutier) and St-Gilles-Croix-de-Vie 45min. Aeroplane service from Bouin and La Roche-sur-Yon (information, tel 51 62 31 65). Helicopter from Fromentine (Oya Hélicoptères, tel : 51 59 22 22).

Market : Tuesday and Saturday at Port-Joinville.

Festival : Fête du Thon (tuna-fishing festival), early Aug.

Specialities : Tuna.

Musée Historial. Guided tours explaining the history of the Ile d'Yeu in the house where Marshal Pétain's wife lived during her husband's imprisonment. * 1 July-31 Aug, daily 10am-noon & 4-7pm. Hotel des Voyageurs, Port-Joinville (tel : 51 58 36 88). 20F.

Grand Phare. You get a fantastic view of the island and, on a clear day, as far as Noirmoutier and St-Gilles-Croix-de-Vie from the top of this inland lighthouse slightly to the north-west of the centre (though you will have to climb 201 steps first). Since it is a working concern, it is best to telephone in advance to arrange a convenient time. ‡ School holiday periods between Easter and 31 Oct, daily 10am-noon & 2-5pm (summer 9am-noon & 2-5.30pm). Tel : 51 58 30 61. Free, but the lighthouse-keepers appreciate a tip.

Plongée sous-marine. If you have a British diving licence and health-certificate you can take out temporary membership and join local sub-aqua enthusiasts exploring the rocks and wrecks that surround the coast. ‡ 1 May-1 Nov. Challans Aquatique Club, Rue des Bossilles, Port-Joinville (tel : 51 58 70 00).

CHAPTER 2

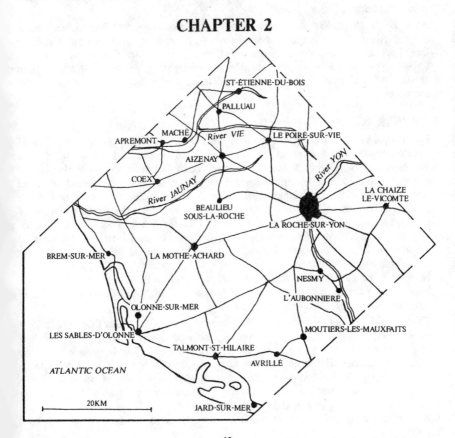

AIZENAY

Pleasant village on the edge of a small forest, 16km north-west of La Roche-sur-Yon. Beside the enormous, early-20th-century church is the Angélus pâtisserie, a paradise for foodies with a sweet tooth, selling the most irresistible cakes, hand-made chocolates and home-made ice-cream. In the local supermarkets you can buy a deliciously fresh, ultra-soft goat's cheese known as a "petit chabi" made nearby at La Robinière, about 4km south-west along the D6.

Market : First and third Mondays of the month.
Festivals : Fête du Millet, mid-August.
Specialities : Millet, goat's cheese.
Brocante : Broc'Ouest (signposted off Route de Challans and Route de Nantes) - two barns full of furniture and bric-à-brac. Wed-Mon 10am-12.30pm & 2.30-7pm, Sun 2.30-7pm.

Forest walks. Marked footpaths starting from the camp-site (signposted to the north of the D948) lead you through glades inhabited by deer and squirrels, a pond full of frogs, and children's play areas ; you may also come across a field of millet, a grain connected in most people's minds with budgies, but which represents here an attempt to revive the taste for a cereal that was once an important part of the local diet (declared by none other than Dr John Kellogg to be the only grain capable of, alone, sustaining human life). ▪

Stèle de la Brionnière. A granite monument beside a country lane, 5.5km south-west of Aizenay, marks the spot where a consignment of arms was parachuted to local Resistance workers on 11 August 1943. To find it, take the D6 towards St-Gilles-Croix-de-Vie, turn left immediately after a level-crossing, on to the D50, then right at the D55 and first right on to a small lane, where there is a signpost to the memorial. ▪

APREMONT

Picturesque village, clinging to the rocky sides of the Vie valley 26km north-west of La Roche-sur-Yon, dominated by a gigantic water-tower and the remains of a Renaissance castle. Around Rue des Bretons, to the south of the river, the narrow streets are lined with a few imposing mansions ; on the north side, smaller houses stagger up the steep slope alongside the church. A dam just east of the castle hill has created a 166-hectare lake - the largest in the Vendée - that attracts lovers of swimming and water-sports from miles around (including a vast proportion of English visitors). Footpaths tempt the energetic, as do the canoe trips on the seaward side of the dam on the river Vie and rock-climbing courses on the cliffs that rise around the edges of the lake.

Festivals : Fête des Battages (old-time rural crafts), mid-July.
Specialities : Traditionally-cured Jambon de Vendée (ham) by G. Petitgas, available in shops and supermarkets throughout the region.

Château d'Apremont. Two towers and a chapel remain of the fine castle built in 1534 by Admiral Philippe Chabot de Brion, a childhood friend of François I who had accompanied the French king at the Field of the Cloth of Gold 14 years earlier. The young King Louis XIII is said to have slept in a first-floor room on 17 April 1622, after defeating the Protestants at Riez. Constructed on the site of an earlier 13th-century stronghold (parts of which still surround the outer courtyard), the castle later fell into disrepair and was partially demolished in 1733.

You can climb its east tower via a series of empty rooms, looking out at each level over the increasingly small rooftops of Apremont, until you reach the top, beneath a magnificent tracery of wooden beams that supports the pointed roof. Back at ground level, follow the signs to the "voûte cavalière", a steep indoor ramp hewn into the rock that could take horsemen from the courtyard level to the water-meadow below. The other interesting feature, half-buried beneath a corner of the garden, is the "glacière" (ice-house) where perishable food was once stored - it still provides a welcome breath of cool air in the height of summer. The more recent buildings that surround the inner courtyard contain the Mairie, the local fire brigade, and occasional art exhibitions. Sometimes, on summer nights, you may catch an open-air theatrical or other performance. ▪ First Sat of month 10.30am-12.30pm & 1-6.30pm (15 Mar-15 May, Sat, Sun & public holidays 10.30am-12.30pm & 1-6.30pm ; 15 May-30 Sept, daily 10.30am-12.30pm & 1-6.30pm). Tel : 51 55 27 18. 12F (or 15F, which includes a visit to the water tower - see below).

Salle Panoramique. Let yourself be whisked by lift up the 80m-high water tower for a stupendous view westward to the sea and islands, eastward towards plain and "haut-bocage". Choose a clear day, and take binoculars and a map for an interesting exercise in orientation. ⌗ 1 June-30 Sept, daily 10.30am-1pm & 1.30-6.30pm. Route de Maché (tel : 51 55 27 18). 15F (admits also to the castle).

Lake. One of the major summer attractions for the locals, and therefore particularly crowded on Sundays and bank holidays, this is nevertheless a delightful spot with an (imported) sandy beach, trees, fishing, safe swimming, summer-season hire of sailing dinghies, pedaloes, windsurfers and rowing boats, plus a cheerful restaurant with mini-golf. Many would-be windsurfers prefer to make their first splashy attempts here, rather than in the open sea. ▪

L'AUBONNIERE

If you are intrepid enough to follow "gîte d'étape" (accommodation for hikers) signs leading east off the narrow lane between Chaillé-sous-les-Ormeaux and Le Champ-St-Père (some 14km south-east of La Roche-sur-Yon), you reach a carefully renovated set of honey-coloured buildings that have been turned into a hostel and small museum.

Le Grand Rochereau. Wander down the path to a magical spot where the fast-flowing river Yon tumbles over weirs and swirls around alder trees and granite boulders. A string of watermills used to be powered by the current - but now it is quite a challenge to make out their ruins, heavily shrouded in ivy. Some parts of the bank are pretty steep, particularly if you walk to the right, so hold securely on to any small children. If you cross the river by footbridge and turn to the north the path takes you alongside a boar farm. ▪

AVRILLÉ

This village, 23km east of Les Sables d'Olonne - together with that of Le Bernard, 6km to the south-east - contains an incredible amount of prehistoric remains. The 23 dolmens and 100 menhirs that sprout from the ground have earned the area the nickname of "the Carnac of the Vendée" (after the megalith-rich village in Brittany). The tourist office organises guided visits to some of the sites, and provides maps for those wishing to tour by bike, by car or on foot. Even without leaving the village you will find one of the largest standing-stones in France - the 7m "menhir du camp de César" - dwarfing visitors to the garden behind the Mairie.

Château de la Guignardière. Such a well-preserved Renaissance stately home is a rare sight in the Vendée, but La Guignardière, about 1km west of the village, has survived because it was occupied by the "Bleus" or Republican forces during the civil war and thus escaped damage. Its origins go back to 1538 when the elegant slate-roofed castle was built by Jean Girard, baker to the French king François I. It is pleasant to picnic in the park, beside the long artificial lake or in the woods, where no fewer than 14 menhirs of varying sizes are concealed among the trees. Guided tours of the castle's interior reveal a staircase (pierced, at one point, with a hole through which defenders could shoot at any enemy coming up the stairs), an incredibly complex network of beams that hold up the roof, and picturesque, vaulted cellars that run beneath the whole area of the house above. * Mid-June-mid-Sept, daily 10am-6.30pm. Tel : 51 22 30 70. 30F (grounds only, 15F), students and children 23F, children under 10 free.

CAIRN. Archaeological neolithic research centre, 3.5km south-west of Avrillé. As well as conventional digging and dating, the resident archaeologists looking into the world of prehistoric man arrange a fascinating summer programme offering demonstrations of flint-tool making, stone-polishing, weaving, pottery and basket-work, as practised 5,000 years ago, and invite visitors to try ancient techniques for lighting fires, making toys and raising or moving huge stones. ‡ Easter holidays, daily 3-6pm ; 10 May-29 Sept, Sun, Wed & public holidays 3-6pm (8 July-7 Sept, Mon 2.30-7pm, Tues-Sun 10am-12.30pm & 2.30-7pm). St-Hilaire-la-Forêt (tel : 51 33 38 38). 35F, children 10F.

Dolmen de la Frébouchère. Follow the signs from near the Romanesque church in the village of Le Bernard, 6km south-east of Avrillé. In the heart of the surrounding countryside you will be led to the largest known prehistoric burial-chamber in the Vendée, the top slab of which weighs 100 tonnes. Even though the area around it has been prettied up with a rather incongruous pink gravel path, this huge dolmen remains a magnificent and stirring sight. ■

BEAULIEU-SOUS-LA-ROCHE

Picturesque village, clustered around a tree-shaded square, 19km west of La Roche-sur-Yon.

Festivals : Foire à l'Ancienne (old-time street fair), late July ; Foire à la Brocante (two-day antiques fair), early August.

Crafts : Stoneware pottery by Marie-Christine Grangiens, at La Cantardière, 3km north of the village (tel : 51 98 88 22).

BREM-SUR-MER

Village, once a seaside port, 29km north of Les Sables-d'Olonne. Dolmens and menhirs that dot the area show that civilisation began here at least 5,000 years ago. There is fishing in the river Auzance and walks through the pine forest to the south. At nearby St-Nicolas-de-Brem, as well as visiting its ancient church (see below), you can make out a mound on which once stood a fortress built more than a thousand years ago to repel marauding pirates.

It may seem strange to think of sea-breezes wafting over vineyards, but there are no fewer than 13 in the area, producing red, white and rosé wines served, it is said, at the table of Cardinal Richelieu and today marketed under the Fiefs Vendéens label.

Market : Tuesday and Friday.

Specialities : Oysters, VDQS Fiefs Vendéens wines (white, red and rosé).

Festivals : Broc-à-Brem (antiques market), late July.

Église St-Nicolas-de-Brem. Just off the main road to the north-west of Brem you come across a real delight, the remains of the Romanesque church built by monks from St Martin's monastery near Tours in 1020. Of its original three naves, just the central one has survived destruction by the Protestants during the Wars of Religion. The ancient, carved façade above the west door, famous throughout France, is thought to show St Nicholas ; two intertwined, fire-breathing snakes decorate the top of a small window on the south side. The simple, whitewashed interior has little decoration, but the remains of some 12th-century frescoes were revealed in the early 1980s, languishing beneath layers of paint : on the left, a crucifixion ; on the right, a scene of three women visiting Christ's tomb after the Resurrection. ■

Musée du Vin. Wine museum on the south-east edge of the village (on the D38), giving the history and traditions of the local vineyards and offering tastings of the local wines of Brem. ⚏ Easter-14 June, Mon-Sat 2.30-7.30pm ; 15 June-15 Sept, Mon-Sat 9.30am-12.30pm & 2.30-7.30pm. Moulin de Bellevue, Route de l'Ile d'Olonne (tel : 51 90 56 28). Free.

Parc d'attractions des Dunes. Roundabouts for younger children and exciting rides for older ones at this amusement park near the beach of Les Dunes, just on the north side of Brem, on the D38. ⚏ Easter-15 Sept, Sat, Sun 2-8pm (1-30 June, daily 2-8pm ; 1 July-31 Aug, daily 10am-8pm). Rue de l'Écours (tel : 51 90 54 29). 25F.

Dolmens and menhirs. North-west of Brem and to the west of the roundabout on the D38 you glimpse a somewhat collapsed dolmen on the track that then runs parallel to the coast, leading to La Normandelière beach. Other prehistoric stones are the Menhir de la Crulière (down a track to the north of the D54 about 2km east of Brem), and the Menhir de la Conche Verte (which you can find if you follow the GR364 footpath into the pine forest of Olonne, to the south of Brem). ■

Église de la Chaize-Giraud. Although the interior of this Romanesque church 5km north of Brem has been heavily restored after near-terminal damage during the

Revolution, it retains much of its original atmosphere. The west front is all that remains of the 12th-century construction ; on the façade you can make out, on the right, the Adoration of the Kings and, on the left, the Annunciation by Gabriel to the Virgin Mary. The sculptures look a bit moth-eaten, but then they are 800 years old. Some delightfully-carved stone faces adorn the roof-line and the imposing doorway. ▪

Mini-Golf. A good, 18-hole, crazy-golf course at Brétignolles, 4km north-west of Brem, can provide a couple of hours of fun for all the family as they play their way around the amusing obstacles. To find it, turn west off the D38 at the roundabout with the D40, that leads towards the seafront and the central square of Bretignolles. The mini-golf is a few hundred yards along the road, on the left, behind a white wire fence. ♯ Easter-30 Sept, Sat, Sun 2-6pm (15-30 June, daily 2-6pm ; 1 July-31 Aug, daily 9.30am-noon & 2-10pm). Rue de la Parée, Brétignolles-sur-Mer. 18F

Havre de la Gachère. Out-of-season visitors can find an area of miraculously unspoilt sand dunes about 3km south of Brem. Take the road that runs parallel to the new D80 and turn right immediately you have crossed the bridge over the river Auzance at Gachère, following the sign to the Plage des Dunes. The lane winds across the sandy expanse to finish on the coast by a couple of stone jetties which protect the mouth of the river. ▪

LA CHAIZE-LE-VICOMTE

Large village, 8.5km east of La Roche-sur-Yon on the D948 towards Ste-Hermine, containing the Vendée's largest Romanesque church (see below). Surrounding it are some pleasant rural lanes and a stream.

Market : Third Tuesday of the month.

Festivals : Fête des Chasseurs (game fair), late August.

Riding : One-day rides (picnic provided) in the forest of La Chaize 5km south-east of the village, for groups of 4-10 at around 300F per person. Ferme Équestre de la Batardraie, Fougeré (tel : 51 05 72 41).

Église St-Nicolas. Look out for signs pointing off to the south of the main road because this enormous, 900-year-old granite church with its 16th-century fortifications is somewhat hidden away. The columns lining its austere, Norman-style nave are topped with interesting carvings. ▪

COEX

Attractive village 25km west of La Roche-sur-Yon. As well as lining its main street with pink paving-slabs, and futuristic bollards that double as street-lighting, the council has resolved to make Coëx a centre for floral decoration - putting the emphasis on plants with interesting fragrances.

Market : Saturday.

Festivals : Carnival, mid-Lent ; Foire à la brocante (antiques fair), late April. At L'Aiguillon-sur-Vie, 6km south-west, Foire aux pinceaux (art festival, with artists setting up their easels in the street), early August.

Golf : Golf des Fontenelles. Particularly suitable for comparative newcomers to the game is this 6,185-metre course, 5km south-west of Coëx (see page 15 for details of Vendée Golf Pass). L'Aiguillon-sur-Vie (tel : 51 54 13 94). ▪

Riding : Centre Equestre de l'Étoile. Large, well-equipped establishment 3km west of Coëx. Route de St-Gilles (tel : 51 54 71 23). ▪

Parc Philippe Perrocheau. Behind the picturesque Mairie on the main street is the village's pride - a large, flower-filled park that includes an "olfactorium", a perfume trail of labelled plants with intense scents, ranging from the everyday odours of geraniums and roses to more unusual aromas of aniseed, chocolate and even tar. Descriptive brochures are available from the little cabin by the pond, where swans glide by and fountains shoot into occasional spurts of activity.

Children are bound to enjoy the ingenious "Rigole aux fleurs", a cross between mini-golf and "Snakes & Ladders" that has been created along the edges of the borders : red holes make you lose time ; green ones let you leap ahead ; yellow ones are "safe". Even grown-ups will learn something ; all holes have names and descriptions of plants that can be seen around you - in French, so you have a language lesson as well as a horticultural one. (Clubs and balls can be rented from the cabin : 20F, children 10F.) A children's play area includes slides emerging from a Japanese-style hut. Occasional concerts and spectacles are held in the park. ▪ Daily (mini-golf 1 June-15 Sept), 10am-8pm. Tel : 51 54 28 80. 30F, children free (1 Nov-31 May, free).

Lac du Jaunay. Picturesque, tree-lined lake 2km south of Coëx - invisible from the surrounding road network. One of the prettiest places to make for is La Baudrière, about 5km south of Coëx, which has the atmosphere of a seaside fishing village and where, in summer, you can rent canoes, pedaloes and mountain-bikes. The bridge near here is the only crossing-point over the water. ▪

Karting et Quad. Children and adults alike can enjoy go-karting (from the age of 7) or riding four-wheeled "quad" bikes (from the age of 4) at this circuit 4km west of Coëx. ▪ Sat, Sun 2pm-dusk (1 May-30 Sept, daily 10am-8pm ; 1-31 July, daily 10am-10pm ; 1-31 Aug, daily 10am-9.30pm). St Révérend (tel : 51 54 66 93). Karts : 45F for 6 mins, children 30F ; quad bikes : 50F for 10 mins, children 35F.

La Roseraie de Vendée. Just off the D6, at a crossroads 4km west of Coëx, lies this recently-planted garden that exhibits 8,000 roses (500 varieties) within its 3 hectares. The shop sells rose-flavoured jams, liqueurs, syrup and other goodies. Guided tours available in the mornings. ⌗ 1 May-30 Nov, daily 9.30am-7pm. Carrefour des 4 Chemins, St-Révérend (tel : 51 55 24 03). 10F, children free.

JARD-SUR-MER

This village 20km east of Les Sables-d'Olonne has been left high and dry, almost 2km from the sea. The church of Ste-Radégonde harbours a few Romanesque features to indicate its 11th-century origins - the tourist office offers weekly guided tours of the building in July and August. The village's other notable monument is the 12th-century Abbey of Lieu-Dieu (see below), set 2km to the west of the village where it towers over the unspoilt agricultural buildings that surround it. Market : Monday.

L'Abbaye Notre-Dame de Lieu-Dieu. Richard Coeur-de-Lion, King of England and Duke of Aquitaine, founded this Cistercian abbey 800 years ago. After a long period of prosperity, it suffered greatly in the Hundred Years' War and was further ruined by Protestants during the Wars of Religion. The unusual building, embellished at one end by slate-roofed octagonal turrets, has only recently been restored to a state where the chapter-house, the staircase and the monks' former dormitory can be opened to visitors. (Guided tours daily in July and August, 10am-noon & 2-6pm ; 11F, children 4F.) ▪

Maison de Clemenceau. An enchanting little low-built cottage on the sands, 2km south-east of Jard, where the fiery politician Georges Clemenceau (1841-1929) spent the last 10 years of his life (see also Mouilleron-en-Pareds, page 76 and Mouchamps, page 91).

After his momentous work on the Treaty of Versailles that brought to an end the First World War, he retired here to write his memoirs, overlooking the ocean. The interior, full of books, clothes, furniture and objects, is just as the "Tiger" might have left it to go out for a stroll round his beloved garden with his friend the Impressionist painter Claude Monet (who gave him a hand with its design, though you wouldn't guess it now), or for a chat with visiting dignitaries like the young Hirohito. (If you have to wait before the guide takes you round, use the time to swot up the English notes on the house.) ■ Wed-Mon 9.30am-12.30pm & 2-6pm (1 July-31 Aug, daily 9.30am-12.30pm & 2-7pm). St-Vincent-sur-Jard (tel : 51 33 40 32). 20F

MACHÉ

The casual passer-by would hardly suspect this small lakeside village off the D948, 24km north-west of La Roche-sur-Yon, to be one of the world's leading quail-rearing centres, yet it exports the tiny table-ready birds to shops and restaurants as far away as Japan. (In the offices of one of the three local enterprises hangs a certificate declaring one of its quails to have set a Guinness record at a weight of 363g.)

Always forward-thinking, the locals are now looking into ostrich-farming - you can spy a field full of the haughty-looking creatures if you glance south across a small valley from the D948, between the Maché turning and the road to Le Fougerais, about 1km farther north-west. "Autruche" (ostrich meat), which is strangely fillet-steak-like in both colour and texture, is often on the menu at the friendly Le Fougerais restaurant.

Lake. The edge of the 166-hectare lake may be reached at a peaceful spot for walking, fishing or just contemplating, via Rue du Moulin-à-Eau on a sharp bend in the village. Near the road bridge on Rue du Lac (the D50, signposted from the village centre to Aizenay) there is entertainment between Easter and mid-October : a good 18-hole mini-golf, children's playground, and hire of pedaloes and rowing-boats. ■

Festivals : Fête de la Caille (afternoon events, plus mass quail barbecue in the evening), late July ; Fête du Lac (games and fireworks), 15 August.

Specialities : Quail.

Crafts : Clogmaking.

LA MOTHE-ACHARD

Large village midway between La Roche-sur-Yon and Les Sables-d'Olonne with an interesting turn-of-the-century market-hall made of iron and blue glass.

Market : Friday.

Musée La Roue Tourne. Don't be put off by the unprepossessing exterior of this museum. Inside is a fascinating, idiosyncratic collection, based initially on one man's passion for old perambulators and pushchairs, but now extended to embrace early radio-sets and bikes, plus domestic paraphenalia in room-settings so that you begin to understand the uses of those weird items you come across in brocante shops.

The owner's eyes mist over as he points out to English visitors the merits of the upright, no-nonsense Raleigh bicycle or the graceful Silver Cross pram ; other baby transporters are elegant in wickerwork, low and chunky like a small 1940s car, or streamlined in space-age plastic. ✠ Easter to 31 Oct, Sun & public holidays 2-7pm (1 June-31 Aug, daily 2-7pm). Rue de la Gare (tel : 51 38 65 85 or 51 94 79 16). 15F

MOUTIERS-LES-MAUXFAITS

The pride of this delightful village 21km south of La Roche-sur-Yon is its 18th-century market hall whose tiled roof rests on 41 stalwart stone columns and an intricate structure of solid oak beams. As you might guess from the generally good state of preservation of the houses clustered around the market building and the Romanesque church of St-Jacques, the town shared Republican sympathies during the Wars of the Vendée and thus escaped relatively unscathed.

Market : Friday.

Lac du Graon. Sailing and fishing (but no swimming) are permitted in this lake at St-Vincent-sur-Graon, 5km north-east of Moutiers. ▪

Arboretum. Rare species of trees and shrubs in a 2-hectare garden 5km north-west of Moutiers. Particularly strong on variegated plants. * 1 Mar-1 Nov, daily 9am-7pm. St-Avaugourd-des-Landes (tel : 51 98 90 11). 10F (guided tour 15F).

NESMY

Village 6km south of La Roche-sur-Yon, known for the pottery industry (see below) that has made use of the local clay deposits since the 13th century.

Festivals : Fête des Vendanges (festival of new wine), early October.

Crafts : Pottery.

Golf : Golf de la Domangère. A 6,480-metre, California-style course of dramatic challenges near La Roche-sur-Yon, designed around a 15th-century mansion that is now a hotel and clubhouse. The seventh hole is the longest in France (see page 15 for details of Vendée Golf Pass). Route de Nesmy, 85310 Nesmy (tel : 51 07 60 15). ▪

Vieille Poterie. Monsieur Charpentreau's family has been working this pottery since 1867 - the old coal-fired kilns, now abandoned in favour of gas-fired ones, stand around in different stages of decay. Inside the rickety buildings, the clay-spattered workshops are a hive of industry. A pleasantly chaotic shop sells the hand-turned and hand-painted products that range from pretty, flower-decorated plates, candlesticks, jugs and dishes to traditional, 60-litre salt-glazed storage jars ideal for vinegar-making, or for holding a lifetime's supply of gherkins. Descriptive leaflet available in English. ▪ Shop : Mon-Sat 10am-noon & 2-6.30pm, Sun 2.30-6.30pm. Tel : 51 07 62 57.

OLONNE-SUR-MER

Large village, now stranded 2km from the sea, 5km north of Les Sables-d'Olonne.

Festivals : Fête du vin nouveau (festival of new wine), early September.

Golf : Golf des Olonnes. There are plenty of water features on this 6,127-metre course just to the east of the village, suitable for all levels of player (see page 15 for details of Vendée Golf Pass). Olonne-sur-Mer (tel : 51 33 16 16). ▪

Mémoire des Olonnes. Museum of local costume, customs and way of life in an old house behind the enormous village church. ♯ 15 June-15 Sept, Thurs-Sat 4-7pm (1 July-31 Aug, Wed-Sat 4-7pm). 1 Rue Paul Bert (tel : 51 90 75 45). Free.

Observatoire d'oiseaux. Signposted off the D38, 2km north of Olonne and just before you reach the village of Ile d'Olonne, this wooden birdwatching post overlooks the river Vertonne and the old salt marshes. Telescopes are installed at opening times, when you are assisted in identifying the avocets and other birds that wade in this wetland, though there is nothing to stop you turning up on other days to enjoy the view on your own. ▪ First Sun of month 2-6pm (1 July-31 Aug, daily 9.30am-noon &

3-7pm). Ile d'Olonne (tel : 51 33 12 97). Free. (In summer you can also view the surrounding area from the quaintly-shaped tower of Ile d'Olonne church.)

Olona Parc. Miniature train, games, inflatables and 50 other attractions for children. ♯ 1 May-mid-Oct, Sat, Sun 10.30am-7pm (mid-June-mid-Sept, daily 10am-10pm). D32 - Route de Challans (tel : 51 33 12 45). 35F.

PALLUAU

Large village 22km north-west of La Roche-sur-Yon, with some grand slate-roofed houses lining its main street. In the Middle Ages tens of thousands of pilgrims from Britain and Brittany, with their staffs and their cockle-shells, passed through this and other places en route to northern Spain and the shrine of St James at Santiago de Compostela (see page 20). Today some of their ancient tracks through the Vendée have been researched and are being signposted as footpaths, with Palluau at their heart (where a hostel accommodates today's walkers).

Exposition sur les Pèlerins de St-Jacques. A fascinating exhibition about the investigations into the pilgrim routes : names of fields, hamlets and villages are vital clues - those containing James or Jacques, or "abbaye" or "maladrerie" (hospital) hint at sites of monastic settlements that sprung up between the 10th and 12th centuries to care for the physical and spiritual needs of pilgrims. ♯ 15 June-30 Sept, daily 10am-12.30pm & 3-6pm. Free.

Château de Palluau. Ravaged in 1794 during the Wars of the Vendée, this once-proud medieval building is now just a substantial ruin that can be glimpsed in the woods to the east of the Relais St-Jacques. You can take a grassy footpath (follow it straight on, rather than bearing left into private territory) for a closer view across the dried-out moat. ∎

LE POIRÉ-SUR-VIE

Attractive village perched on a rocky outcrop 13km north-west of La Roche-sur-Yon, the hub of a network of footpaths. One or two fine Renaissance-style houses look on to the picturesque main square. In some of the fields around the village during the autumn you sometimes see strange piles of vegetation stacked around single poles. This is the harvest of the ubiquitous mogettes, the small white haricot beans that are still a staple food of the Vendeans, and which appear in many menus, often accompanying local gammon. At the annual festival you may catch sight of members of the Brotherhood of the Mogette in their bizarre costume of bean-pod white, covered by a green cloak (representing the plant's leaves), and topped with a white, bean-shaped hat.

Market : Thursday, Saturday and Sunday.
Festivals : Nuit de la Mogette (a lakeside beanfeast), mid-August.
Specialities : Mogettes.
Crafts : Woven fabrics by Monique Biron, at La Micherie, 5km west of Le Poiré (tel 51 31 85 78).

Moulin à Elise. A 19th-century watermill - one of at least seven that once existed in the district - recently restored to working order. The large waterwheel creaks round while a guide gives a 15-minute explanation of the process, with the aid of a complex diagram showing the to-ings and fro-ings the wheat undergoes before emerging as bags of flour. You can climb the stairs for a look at the hopper feeding the millstone with grain. Little bags of both ordinary and "blé noir" (buckwheat) flour are on sale in the shop. Nearby are picnic tables, footpaths and a crêperie. ⊞ 1 May-30 Sept, Sun & public holidays 2-7pm (1 July-31 Aug, Fri-Mon 2-7pm). Tel : 51 31 61 38. 10F, children free.

Aux P'tites Puces. Not, strictly speaking, on the tourist circuit, but a visit to these two huge warehouses, selling every conceivable type of fabric by the *kilogram*, is an unmissable experience for anyone who knows how to thread a needle. If you have ever wondered where to buy material to make macintoshes, or how to get those odd bits to repair dungaree or bra straps, this self-service Aladdin's cave is the answer. It also offers bedspreads, "bleus de travail" (blue workman's overalls), cast-iron fire-backs and even wire-netting. Stock changes fast, as much of it is end-of-range stuff. ■ Thurs-Sat 9.30am-12.30pm & 2.30-6.45pm. Route d'Aizenay (tel : 51 06 49 50).

Sentier des Farfadets. As well as the 70km GR Entre Vie et Yon, you can try other shorter, circular trails like this one that starts 3km west of the town and leads along sunken lanes, lined with trees and prickly butcher's broom, to a huge, 15-ton megalithic boulder - called variously the Pierre des Farfadets (the Goblins' Stone) or the Pierre de la Merlière - on which you can make out some of the 300-odd mysterious signs that have been engraved on it by prehistoric (or fairy) hands, though some say they are the fingermarks of Gargantua, Rabelais' legendary giant (see page 73), who used it for playing marbles. Near La Planche au Gravier - a ford at the western extremity of this 6km circuit - is a pleasant picnic spot by a stream. Maps of local walks are available from the tourist office in Le Poiré ; there is also one fixed to a board at the Planche au Gravier car park. ■

Chapelle Ste-Radégonde. In the depths of the countryside, 3km south of Le Poiré and signposted off the road north of the village of La Genétouze, stands an small chapel, rebuilt in 1863 on the site of a much older one, dedicated to a 6th-century saint who was once a queen of France. According to legend, Radégonde was fleeing from her cruel husband when, at this quiet spot, she came across a peasant sowing oats. Desperate to avoid capture, she besought him to say, if asked whether the queen had passed by, that no one had been that way since he had started to sow. He agreed, whereupon the seeds he had sown grew instantly, high enough to hide the fugitive queen. Her husband, witnessing this miracle, recognised the hand of God, and abandoned his pursuit. Unfortunately the door is generally locked, but the setting is picturesquely wooded, and you can walk down a muddy path to the stream that runs below. A pilgrimage takes place in mid-August. ■

LA ROCHE-SUR-YON

After the Wars of the Vendée, Napoleon Bonaparte wished to create a new capital for the unruly Vendée (having decided that the existing one of Fontenay-le-Comte was too far away from the centre) and picked on the small village of La Roche-sur-Yon in 1804. Demolishing much of the old part (though a glimpse of it can still be seen round Place de la Vieille Horloge), he created a "new town" of Classical-style buildings and die-straight streets around the central parade-ground, from which radiated avenues designed to give 20,000 soldiers instant access to any trouble-spots. Modestly, he called it "Napoléon". With the fluctuating status of France over the next 66 years the town's name was changed no fewer than seven times, reverting finally to that of the original village in 1870. (From the platform of the railway station, you can still read an earlier one - "Napoléon-Vendée" - etched firmly into the stone, the name the town bore under Napoléon III at the time the railway arrived in the 1860s.) The lack of interesting nooks and crannies that the grid layout imposed helped earn

La Roche the unwelcome description of "about the dullest town in France" from the 19th-century travel writer John Murray. However, efforts have been made since to liven up its image. A witty fountain of oil drums now makes a splash in front of the theatre; the few old buildings around Place de la Vieille Horloge have been restored ; and in the height of summer you can sip a drink at the café in the Jardin de la Mairie to the accompaniment of jazz music and other entertainment.

Principal shopping areas are Rue Georges-Clemenceau and its offshoots, and the pedestrianised streets around Rue des Halles, west of the market (a modern concrete bunker hidden away behind the large Classical-style church on Place Napoléon). If you are desperate for Marmite, marmalade or Weetabix you will find these and many other British specialities at a shop called Le Comptoir Irlandais, between the church and the market. Junk-shop fantatics should not miss Emmaüs (see below), where three floors of a warehouse are filled with a changing selection of furniture, books and objects.

A signposted "Circuit Napoléon" leads you on a 2.5km hike around some of the most obvious sights ; farther afield you can embark on some of the "Sentiers de la Fragonnette" (a series of walks around beauty spots on the town's perimeter), or the 70km GR circuit Entre Vie et Yon. Maps of all these are available from the tourist office in Rue du Maréchal Joffre, part of the Galerie Bonaparte complex, off Place Napoléon.

Market : Tuesday, Thursday and Saturday (the busiest day). A large, open-air market in Place Napoléon on the second Monday of the month.

Brocante : Emmaüs (part of a highly-successful network set up by Abbé Pierre, an elderly French priest, to sell donated goods and to be run by, and on behalf of, down-and-outs), 34 Rue Paul Doumer, Tues, Wed, Fri 2.30-6pm, Sat 9am-noon & 2.30-6pm. Le Mobilier d'Occasion (by railway tracks), 163 Boulevard Louis-Blanc, Tues-Sat 10am-noon & 3-7pm. Le Grenier Yonnais (by level-crossing on the D948), 110bis Rue Jacques Cartier, Tues-Fri 3-7pm, Sat 9am-12.30pm & 3-7pm. At Bourg-sous-la-Roche (2km east, on the D948) a flea market is held near the church on the second Sunday morning of the month.

Haras National. This stud - one of the largest in France - was founded by Napoleon in 1843 to breed horses for his army. Today its roomy boxes are home to around 100 stallions of various breeds - from draught horses (mostly for maintaining the country's horse-meat trade) to elegant riding horses and thoroughbred trotters. The guide on the one-hour tour of this impeccably-kept city farm, explains how the resident animals are exercised, shod, and generally cared for (and lets you stroke a few of them, too). From February to July most of the stallions are stationed away in different corners of the Vendée to cover mares elsewhere. ⌗ 1 July-31 Aug, Mon-Fri 10am-noon & 2.30-4.30pm (closed on public holidays) ; 1 Sept-31 Jan, Mon-Fri 2.30-4.30pm. Boulevard des États-Unis (tel : 51 37 01 85). 15F

Maison des Métiers. Attractively-restored 18th-century house in the heart of the old town. Its downstairs rooms are filled with high-quality products made by local craft people : clothes, lamps, furniture, pottery and leather goods, all for sale. Upstairs is model of the town as it was before Napoleon laid hands on it, complete with castle. There is a tiny garden behind, accessible from Rue St-Hilaire. ■ Tues-Sat 9.15am-noon & 2.15-6.30pm. Place de la Vieille Horloge (tel : 51 62 51 33). (On the opposite side of the square is the Italianate Maison de la Renaissance, dating from 1566.)

Musée Municipal. Temporary exhibitions on the ground floor; upstairs, passing some archaeological relics on the way, you find a room devoted to portraits by the

19th-century artist Paul Baudry (1828-86) - who was born in La Roche - with works by a few other Victorian-era French artists, and another room centred on René Couzinet (1904-56), a pioneering aircraft designer. Among postcards on sale are some charming reproductions of the work of Benjamin Rabier (1864-1939), another native of the town, who designed the endearing logo for Vache-qui-Rit (Laughing Cow) cheese. In France, he is even better known as the creator of Gédéon, a sort of Gallic Donald Duck, whose cartoon exploits gripped the nation between the wars. ■ Wed-Mon 10am-noon & 2-6pm, Sun 3-6pm. Rue Jean-Jaurès (tel : 51 47 48 50). 15F.

Lac de Moulin-Papon. Lake 2km north of La Roche offering sailing and fishing (but no swimming) ; a footpath (part of the GR Entre Vie et Yon) makes almost a complete circuit of the lake, with pedestrian markers giving details - even in Braille - of local flora to be enjoyed. By car, turn right off the northbound D937 at the big roundabout, then left on the D37, after which you can try various right turns to get down to the water's edge. ■

Abbaye des Fontenelles. Along the N160, 3km south-west of La Roche, is a sign-posted turning to the right leading several kilometres along a lane to a car park at the entrance to a farm. Walk up the drive (murmuring politely to any of the farmer's family) and, looming to your right, are the proud remains of a Romanesque abbey built in 1210, half-hidden among farm buildings and trees. Today only the pigeons have access to the interior of this vast, sober edifice, except for the third Sunday in September when it is open for National Heritage Day. However, you can wander freely around the outside, and glimpse the tracery of its vaulting through the high, glassless windows - binoculars would be useful for studying the grimacing, carved faces that look down from beneath the eaves. ■

LES SABLES-D'OLONNE

By far the most elegant seaside resort in the Vendée, Les Sables offers a vast, gently-shelving beach of ultra-manicured sand and, on the other side of the same spit of land, a busy fishing port lined with good restaurants and narrow, often hilly, streets full of interesting shops. Not only fishermen lived in the little whitewashed houses, Les Sables was also the home of Jean-David Naud, a notorious pirate of the Caribbean seas, known as "Nau l'Olonnois" who mercilessly tortured his victims, and was himself eaten by cannibals in 1671.

Parking can be a problem - meters function relentlessly, even on Sundays and bank holidays. Alternatives are to find a car park, or to make for one of the residential streets behind the eastern end of the beach and look for a free space there. The most glossy shopping areas are in the pedestrianised streets to the east and north of the church. The Remblai (beachfront promenade) is animated on summer evenings with street performers entertaining passers-by in front of the seafront cafés from about 9pm. Small children love the little roundabouts at place de la Liberté, the gardens behind the tourist office.

Market : Halles Centrales (covered central market), daily ; Arago, Boulevard Arago (to the east of the town centre), daily ; Cours Dupont (north-east of the centre), Wednesday and Saturday ; Fish market, Quai Garnier (near tourist office), Mon-Sat 9am-noon & 4.30-6.30pm (closed bank holidays).

Festivals : Fête de la Mer (festival of the sea), mid-August.

Specialities : Tuna, langoustines, sole.

Brocante : Marché aux Puces (regular flea market), late June-early Sept, Friday mornings, Place de la Liberté.

Halles Centrales. Try and enter the central market-hall (on the seaward side of the church of Notre-Dame de Bon-Port) from Rue du Palais. From here you can look down from the peppermint-green and cream painted first-floor level (where local farmers deal in small amounts of home-grown eggs and vegetables) on the colourful mosaic of traders and shoppers picking their way through the tempting produce laid out below. If you glide down the escalator to join them you will find that this market is one of the few places to offer bunches of fresh but out-of-the-ordinary herbs like basil and coriander, plus mirabelle plums and other unusual items. ▪ Daily 9am-12.30pm.

Rue de l'Enfer. This street, off the south side of Rue des Halles and to the west of the central market, has been featured in the French Guinness Book of Records as the narrowest in France. You'll need to breathe in to squeeze along it - the walls on either side do not even allow for the breadth of an average person's shoulders. ▪

Musée de l'Abbaye de Ste-Croix. Delightfully arranged art gallery and museum in one wing of a 17th-century building that was formerly a Benedictine convent. Temporary exhibitions are held on the ground floor; upstairs are interesting modern works, including some charming pictures of Les Sables in the 1920s by Albert Marquet (1875-1947) and a large selection of colourful collages and paintings by Gaston Chaissac (1910-64). Under a network of beams, the roof space on the top floor houses a collection of mixed-media Surrealist works by the Romanian artist Victor Brauner (1903-66), and a museum of costumes, model ships and items relating to the local fishing industry. An excellent prehistoric section displays finds from the surrounding area alongside photographs of the sites. ▪ Tues-Sun 2.30-5.30pm (15 June-30 Sept, daily 10am-noon & 2.30-6.30pm) ; closed on public holidays. Rue de Verdun (tel : 51 32 01 16). 30F, students and children 10F (free on Wednesdays).

Musée des Guerres de Vendée. You need at least some knowledge of the personalities and events of the Wars of the Vendée (see page 24) to get the most out of this museum which has been set up in an attractive 18th-century house between the casino and the fishing port. Most of its displays consist of costumed waxworks portraying the wars' principal characters (a descriptive sheet in English identifies the significant figures). The basement holds the "baddies" (in Vendean terms), the Republican leaders like Kléber (leader of the fearsome Mayençais troops that reinforced the Revolutionary forces), Carrier (who instituted the horrific drowning massacres in the Loire), Boulard (commander of the garrison stationed at Les Sables, where the sands were soaked with the blood of those guillotined on the promenade above), and Hoche, who finally succeeded in drawing up a peace treaty with the Vendean insurgents.

The large first-floor room contains a mass of documents relating to the period of the 1789 Revolution and the war, collected by a local historian Jacques Khanzadian (a further part of his collection in the small room is unrelated to the war). On the second floor, after passing the famous cannon nicknamed "Marie-Jeanne" (a talisman to the "Blancs" once they had captured it from the Republicans), you come face-to-face with some of the Vendean heroes : La Rochejaquelein, d'Elbée, Cathelineau, Stofflet and Charette gathered at an inn ; the dying Lescure with his wife ; a rebel priest saying an open-air Mass ; and Pitt's British troops and those of exiled French aristocrats who were cut down by Hoche's Republican forces during the disastrous invasion attempt of June 1795 at Quiberon in Brittany.

To the left of the museum's entrance hall is a room where you can rifle through an enormous selection of beautiful reproduction French railway posters (you don't have to pay the admission charge to browse through them). ⯂ Mid-Apr-mid-Sept, daily

10am-12.30pm & 3-7pm. 72 Rue Napoléon (tel : 51 21 03 27). 17F, children 13F.

Jardin Zoologique. Beyond the southernmost end of the Remblai (promenade), some 2km from the town centre, is a collection of monkeys, exotic birds, big cats, wallabies and other animals in a tree-filled park alongside the river Tanchet. ▪ Daily 2-6pm (15 Feb-1 Nov, daily 10.30am-noon & 2-6pm ; 1 May-15 Sept, daily 9.30am-7pm). Puits d'Enfer (tel : 51 95 14 10). 45F, children 20F.

Puits d'Enfer. About 2km south-east of the town centre the coastline turns to cliffs and gulleys, eroded by water, where spray is driven up like geysers on stormy days, earning the site its name of "Hell's Well". (Be careful not to stray near the edge in fierce weather conditions.) ▪

Abbaye St-Jean-d'Orbestier. Overlooking the sea are the solid remnants of this 12th-century abbey, 3km south-east of Les Sables along the corniche, or clifftop coast road. Today half-hidden by some school buildings that surround it, the church is gradually being restored, ready to hold summer exhibitions and concerts. ▪

Fishing and sea trips. A half-day jaunt by boat out beyond the lighthouse of Les Barges provides an opportunity to fish with rod and line (provided, along with the bait) for mackerel or sea-bass that you can take home for supper. Reservations are essential. ♯ 1 May-30 Sept, Sat, Sun 6.30-10.30am & 7-11am (1 July-31 Aug, daily 6.30-10.30am & 7-11am). Vedettes Sablaises, Quai Guiné (tel : 51 21 31 43). 120F, children 90F. (The same company offers 50-minute trips round the bay, for which no advance booking is required ; 45F, children 30F.)

"Kifanlo". A working trawler takes up to 12 people to have a brief taste of a fisherman's life on the high seas. ♯ Easter-Oct, daily, 8am-noon, 1.30-4pm or 4pm-6.30pm, Advance booking via tourist office (tel : 51 32 03 28). Four-hour trips, 100F, children 80F (15 June-15 Sept, 115F & 95F) ; $2^1/_2$-hour trips 65F, children 55F (15 June-15 Sept, 75F & 65F).

L'aventure nature. Guided mountain-bike excursions into the countryside around Les Sables. You can opt for the haunting experience of four hours in the marshes as the sun comes up, and enjoy breakfast at a farmhouse en route ; or a full day trip over hill and dale, with farmhouse lunch, going as far as the Lac du Jaunay 20km to the north. ♯ 1 Apr-30 Sept, daily. Olonne Découverte. Book via tourist office (tel : 51 32 03 28). Full day (8.30am-5pm) 350F, children 300F ; half-day (starts an hour before dawn) 230F, children 200F (prices include cycle hire and lunch or breakfast).

La Chaume. Across the channel that links the port with the sea is the picturesque former fishing village of La Chaume. You can drive around to it, or take a short ferry ride across the harbour mouth from Quai de Guiné on the Les Sables side. The following attractions are located on that side of the channel.

Market : Tuesday, Thursday and Sunday at La Chaume.

Route des Salines. You need to book in advance for this 1hr 45min guided tour by boat, into the marshland, to learn about the salt industry that used to thrive north of Les Sables (an area now largely given over to more profitable oyster-farming). Producing sea-salt may sound romantic, but it's heavy work, opening and closing sluices to let the salt water in, waiting for the heat of summer to evaporate the water, and raking the deposits into large white pyramids under the baking sun. ♯ 1 Apr-31 Oct, days and times vary according to tides. Vendée Port Olona (tel : 51 21 01 19). 52F, children 33F.

Maison du Saunier. A pretty waterside building that was formerly a salt-worker's house lies 1.5km north of La Chaume on the D87a (the museum's name is clearly visible when approaching from the south ; from the opposite direction you will find it just after the ambulance sign on the edge of the village of L'Aubraie). Exhibits include salt-making tools, photographs, and a model of the local salt-pans illustrating methods that have not changed since the time of the Romans. * 15 June-31 Aug, daily 9.30am-noon & 2.30-7pm. 120 Route de l'Aubraie (tel : 51 90 87 74). 20F, children 15F.

Port Olona. Super-chic marina with shops and restaurants, and frequently live music in the bars during the evenings. The port hits the headlines every four years as the start/finish of the gruelling single-handed round-the-world sailing race known as the Vendée-Globe Challenge. This major event is the brainchild of mariner Philippe Jeantot, Les Sables' yachting hero, whose "Crédit Agricole III" can often be seen moored at the quayside. ■

ST-ÉTIENNE-DU-BOIS

If you want to see what a typical small village of the region would have looked like if war had not devastated it, this place, 19km north-west of La Roche-sur-Yon, gives you a good idea. Inexplicably spared by the "colonnes infernales" (see page 27), it has a charming collection of Renaissance houses - one dated 1628 - clustered around the church (though the designer of an ultra-modern Mairie has succeeded, where General Turreau's troops failed, in blighting one side of the square). Stroll around the narrow lanes in the direction of La Mercerie, or take a footpath along the banks of the Boulogne river and across a little ford.
Specialities : Gros-Plant wine.

Chapelle de la Tullévrière. A cockerel and a cross decorate the roof of this chapel in a hamlet 5km north-east of St-Etienne on the D94. It was rebuilt in 1835 on the site of an earlier building where one of the rebel priests (see page 25) celebrated Mass during the Wars of the Vendée. The simplicity of the interior is moving ; two of the stained-glass windows show clandestine religious services of the time, and on the wall is a memorial to 22 local martyrs - men, women and children - slaughtered by the "Bleus" in 1794 as they attempted to hide nearby. ■

TALMONT-ST-HILAIRE

A former port of great charm, nestling at the foot of impressive medieval castle ruins, that once belonged to the powerful Princes of Talmont and, between 1152 and 1204, to the English crown. It was also an important staging-post on the pilgrim routes that led the faithful to the shrine of St James at Santiago de Compostela in northern Spain. Up the hill behind the castle are some beautiful old, ivy-covered houses whose gardens can be glimpsed through the gateways in their high walls. Between July and September the tourist office organises visits to the salt marshes at nearby Querry-Pigeon and La Guittière, where you can also see oyster-rearing, and to the dunes and forest of Le Veillon, 5km to the south-west.
Market : Saturday.
Festivals : Fête de la Vache (old customs, working oxen, milking, butter-making, folk-dancing), early July at Grosbreuil, 9km north of Talmont ; Fête des Huîtres (oyster festival), La Guittière, 2km south of Talmont, mid-July.
Specialities : Oysters.

Château de Talmont. The solidly-built castle remains that you can wander around today are for the most part 12th-century, the work of Richard Coeur-de-Lion (the English king Richard the Lionheart, son of Henry Plantagenet of England and

Eleanor of Aquitaine) who spent a good deal of time hunting in the neighbouring forests. It was much fought over during the Wars of Religion, and reduced to its present state in 1628. From the top of the keep there are marvellous views over the town, the countryside, marshes and sea. In summer you can often take a tour of the castle with a guide in medieval costume. ♯ 1 Mar-15 Nov, daily 9am-noon & 2.30-7pm. Tel : 51 90 27 43. 8F, children 3F.

Musée Automobile de Vendée. Some 6km west of Talmont, this large motor museum contains at least 150 immaculately-presented vehicles dating from 1885 to the 1960s - including such makes as De Dion-Bouton, Bugatti, Hispano-Suiza - and a selection of bicycles, motor-bikes and horse-drawn carriages. ♯ 15 Mar-15 Oct, daily 9.30am-noon & 2-6.30pm (1 June-31 Aug, daily 9.30am-7pm). Tel : 51 22 05 81. 34F, children 15F.

Port-Bourgenay. Spanking-new, traffic-free holiday development and sports complex, 7km south-west of Talmont, built around a marina, with tennis courts, pool and golf-course. ■

Golf : Golf de Port-Bourgenay. A 5,920-metre course laid out beside the coast and around the colourful holiday village (see page 15 for details of Vendée Golf Pass). Tel : 51 22 29 87. ■

CHAPTER 3

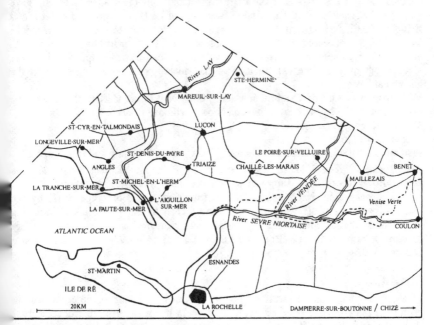

L'AIGUILLON-SUR-MER

Former trading port, 21km south-west of Luçon, at the mouth of the river Lay, where ships once loaded cargoes of the cereals cultivated on the reclaimed land of the "dry" marshes (as the drained area of fenland is known) to the north and north-east. The roads through the village can be extremely crowded in summer, so be prepared for traffic jams if you have to pass this way. You will have plenty of time to study the red British telephone box in the centre of the village (a gift from the town of Burnham-on-Crouch in Essex, with which L'Aiguillon is twinned), and the large pool provided for water-sports.

Fishing and mussel-farming are still the livelihood of those who live in the low, whitewashed cottages - indeed, the bay of Aiguillon is one of the largest shellfish-producing areas of France. Legend has it that a shipwrecked Irishman named Patrick Walton was the first to try planting a stake in the water to encourage mussels to grow on it in 1255, after he found them clinging to posts where he had attached a net for catching birds. Today, as the tide falls, hundreds of thousands of these "bouchots" are revealed standing in the mud, each one holding a rich crop of shellfish that have anchored themselves to it.

Another sort of fishing is practised by the locals on the bridge that links L'Aiguillon to La Faute-sur-Mer. As on many other estuaries in the region, curious constructions of bent poles and square nets - known as "carrelets" - are winched down into the rising tide in the hope of bringing up a harvest of eels, shrimps and other edible delicacies. In July and August you can visit the bay's oyster beds (information from L'Aiguillon tourist office).

You can reach the Pointe de l'Aiguillon - a long spit of land that juts out into Aiguillon Bay - by taking a road that runs beside the 6km dyke built a century ago by Dutch engineers to protect the hard-won fields from the sea. From it you have views on the eastern side of the wind-carved cliffs of La Dive - a small, former island rising to the dizzy height of 15m above the flat fields - and, to the south and south-west, of La Rochelle and the Ile de Ré. Because of the high, crumbling concrete wall, you do not get a view on the seaward side, but you can clamber up primitive steps sticking out of it at intervals to look at the mussel-posts stretching away to the horizon at low tide.

Vast quantities of avocets and other wading birds visit the mud-flats of the Anse de l'Aiguillon (as the bay is known) which is now a wildfowl reserve.

Market : Tuesday and Friday.

Specialities : Mussels, oysters, eels.

Festivals : Courses aux baleinières (whaling-boat races), mid-July and mid-August.

Aux P'tites Puces. Like its equivalent in Le Poiré-sur-Vie (see page 52), this emporium is more of a shopping experience than a tourist attraction. You can purchase every conceivable type of fabric (much of it end-of-range stuff) by the *kilogram* - just snip off what you want and take it to the scales. It's an amazing source of material, whether for upholstery, summer frocks, mackintoshes or lace curtains. ■ Zone artisanale, Route de Luçon (tel : 51 56 46 97). Thurs-Sat 9.30am-12.30pm & 2.30-6.45pm.

ANGLES

This small village, 20km west of Luçon, is worth a detour in order to see the primitive, pockmarked bear sculpture that peers down on visitors from the roof above the west door of its celebrated 12th-century church (see below). Local legend says it was a dangerous animal that abducted and ate young and beautiful women before being turned to stone by a holy man.

Market : Saturday.

Festival : Fête de l'ours (bear festival), late July.

Romanesque church. This handsome building arouses a great deal of interest for the way in which its interior bridges the Romanesque and the later Plantagenet styles. The ribs and curves of the vaulting in the nave show clearly the chunky, rounded arches characteristic of the 12th century alongside some of the finer, more graceful architecture that was to follow.

Several of the tops of the columns are decorated with leaf designs, and there are three interesting statues.

The simply-carved figure high above the nave is thought to represent Henri Plantagenêt (King Henry II of England, who reigned from 1154 to 1189) ; the two more sophisticated works are said to be of his wife, Eleanor of Aquitaine, and of their son Richard Cœur-de-Lion (King Richard I of England) who is known to have spent a large amount of time in the area.

Interspersed with hunting excursions into the forests, Richard the Lionheart built the castle of Talmont, 16km to the north-west (see page 58), and provided the funds for the construction of the Abbey of Lieu-Dieu at Jard, 15km to the west (see page 49).

Beneath a huge wooden trapdoor set in the floor of the nave are steps that lead down to an exceptionally deep, but bare, crypt. ▪

Tour de Moricq. Marooned in the marshland 2km east of Angles rises a huge, isolated square tower, built in the 15th century on what was then the coast, to defend the mouth of the river Lay. During the Wars of Religion Protestant prisoners were held in it. It is not well signposted in Moricq itself, but can be found at the eastern end of the village. ▪

Festival : Fête de la Tour de Moricq, early August.

BENET

Large village on the northern edge of the Marais Poitevin or Green Venice, just south of the N148 and 48km east of Luçon, near the border between the Vendée and the neighbouring departement of Deux-Sèvres.

It is best known for its large 15th-century church (see below), the tower of which can be seen from a considerable distance across the flat land.

Although Benet is not actually on the water, you can rent boats nearby to paddle through the canals that criss-cross the picturesque marshes from Coulon (see page 52), 6km south, from Maillezais, 10km to the west (see page 65), or from Le Mazeau, km to the south-west.

Market : Monday.

Église Ste-Eulalie. The imposing structure is principally gothic in style, but is best known for the wonderfully sculpted façade on the west side. The complex decoration is composed of scenes from the Old and the New Testaments, from Adam and Eve to the life of Christ. ▪

CHAILLÉ-LES-MARAIS

Lying 14km south-east of Luçon, this ancient capital of the "dry" marsh (drained inland) area of the Marais Poitevin was once an island - you can admire some of its cliffs along the D25 leading south-east out of the village. Behind the post office a narrow lane leads to a picnic spot from which you can walk to the mysterious mound called the Ilot de Chaillezay, the site of a castle but now empty except for twisted yews and clumps of butchers' broom. Climb to the top for a wonderful view over the flat marshland.

When the estuary that used to cover this area began to silt up, the first drainage work was undertaken in the 13th century by monks from five nearby abbeys. Their name lives on in the Canal des 5 Abbés - the waterway just south of Chaillé that runs roughly north-east/south-west, dividing the fertile, open meadows of the "dry" marsh ("marais desséché") from the mysterious, tree-lined "wet" marshland ("marais mouillé") to the west. Four centuries later, Henri IV and his successor, Louis XIII, brought in Dutch engineers (from whom the Ceinture des Hollandais - the boundary canal between the marshes and the plain, to the north - gets its name).

Brocante : Dépôt-Vente Sud-Vendée, on N137 at entrance to village. Thurs-Sat 2-7pm, Sun 3-7pm.

Maison du Petit Poitou. A living museum - one of six "maisons du parc" in the Marais Poitevin - lying on the N137 just to the south of the village. You can learn about 17th-century drainage techniques and local farming methods, and see some typical livestock of the region : goats, cows, mules and the "baudet du Poitou", a breed of donkey with an incredibly shaggy coat (see Dampierre-sur-Boutonne, page 63). Unusual crafts demonstrated include the making of cowpat fuel that was highly prized for cooking and heating - even the ash that remained was exported to be used as fertiliser. ♯ 1 May-30 Sept, Tues-Sat 10am-noon & 2-7pm. Tel : 51 56 77 30. 15F, children 8F.

CHIZÉ (Deux-Sèvres)

Village 70km east of La Rochelle, on the eastern edge of a forest - the remains of a vast wooded area that covered the whole region in the Middle Ages.

Zoorama Européen. Some 600 European birds and animals live in this zoo park, from wild boar to wading birds, otters to bison, plus reptiles and various rare breeds snatched back from extinction like the baudet (long-haired donkey - see above, and page 63) of Poitou and the aurochs (a wild ox, the ancestor of domestic cattle). In July and August you can take a 45-minute tour of the large enclosures in a horse-drawn wagon. ♯ 1 Feb-31 Dec, Wed-Mon 10am-noon & 2pm-dusk, Sun & public holidays 10am-dusk (1 Apr-30 Sept, Wed-Mon & public holidays 9am-7pm ; 1 May-30 June daily 9am-7pm ; 1 July-31 Aug, daily 9am-8pm). Villiers-en-Bois (tel : 49 76 79 56) 37F, children 17F.

Moulin de Rimbault. Half-hour guided tours of a 17th-century windmill, restored to working order. ♯ 1 May-31 Oct, Sun & public holidays 3-6pm. Beauvoir-sur-Niort (tel : 49 09 73 05). 12F.

COULON (Deux-Sèvres)

Officially categorised as one of "the most beautiful villages of France", this busy little waterside town, 60km south-east of Luçon and 8km west of Niort, really does live up to its classification, with a handsome church, interesting craft shops lining its old streets, and fisherman's houses reflected in the limpid waters of the Sèvre Niortaise river. As you would expect from the capital of the "marais mouillé", the rural paradise of tree-lined waterways known as "Green Venice" (see La Venise Verte, page 69), you can rent traditional, flat-bottomed boats called "plates" from several companies along the quayside and explore the intricate network of small canals, roofed with leafy branches, that lead off the main river like a series of green cathedrals. Prices from around 125F per 6- or 7-seater boat for 1 hour with a guide (who does the paddling) ; 85F for 1 hour without.

Market : Friday and Sunday.

Maison des Marais Mouillés. The history of the "wet" marshland from prehistoric times and explanations of how it was reclaimed from the sea, first by 13th-century monks and later by Dutch engineers. Also featured are the area's wood industry, fishing, and crops - including the mogettes that are such an important element in the Vendean diet. Photographs illustrate how the flat-bottomed boats are used to transport everything - including livestock - to and from the little green fields. ♯ Easter-31 Oct, Tues-Sun 10am-noon & 2-7pm (1 July-31 Aug, daily 10am-7pm). Place de la Coûtume (tel : 49 35 81 04). 18F, children 10F.

Aquarium de la Venise Verte. You can enjoy close-up views of carp, perch and some of the other freshwater fish that normally live in the canals, and see a slide show explaining their habits. Other tanks contain more exotic varieties. ♯ 1 Apr-31 Oct, daily 10am-noon & 2.30-7pm. 10 Place de l'Église (tel : 49 35 90 31). 19F, children 8F.

DAMPIERRE-SUR-BOUTONNE (Charente-Maritime)

Pretty village on the river Boutonne, just south of the forest of Chizé and about 70km east of La Rochelle.

Maison du Baudet du Poitou. An experimental farm, 3km east of Dampierre, that has undertaken a last-ditch attempt to save a unique local breed of donkey from extinction. A guide explains the story of the baudet (a large brown creature with shaggy dreadlocks that sweep the ground) and a video illustrates how the animal was crossed to produce a tough, load-carrying mule. The success of the rescue pro-gramme is apparent from the sight of the 20 pure-bred baudets grazing nearby, and more than 60 cross-bred animals. ■ Daily 9am-noon & 2-7pm. La Tillauderie, Dampierre-sur-Boutonne (tel : 46 24 07 72). 18F, children 10F.

ESNANDES (Charente-Maritime)

Since the 13th century, fishermen from this small village 12km north of La Rochelle have used sturdy, flat-bottomed boats called "acons" to collect their daily harvest of mussels from the thousands of bouchots or stakes planted in the bay (see L'Aiguillon-sur-Mer, page 59). In summer you can climb the tower of the fortified Romanesque church for a superb view over the village and the flat marshes to the north and east.

Speciality : Mussels ; "mouclade" (a creamy dish of mussels).

Maison de la Mytiliculture. The geography and biology of the bay of Aiguillon, and an audio-visual explanation of the methods by which mussels are "farmed". ■ Tues-Sat 10am-12.30pm & 2.30-6pm, Sun 2.30-6pm (15 June-15 Sept, Mon-Sat 10am-7pm, Sun & public holidays 2.30-7pm). Tel : 46 01 34 64. 18F.

LA FAUTE-SUR-MER

Forests of mussel bouchots stretch up and down the coast (see L'Aiguillon-sur-Mer, page 59), 23km south-west of Luçon, across the ripple-marked sands as the tide falls. Thousands of wading birds take advantage of the sheltered environment around the Pointe d'Arçay, 5km to the south-east, a vital staging-point on the migratory routes.

Market : Thursday and Saturday.

Specialities : Oysters and mussels.

Parc de Californie. More than 300 exotic birds including flamingoes, storks, tou-cans, pelicans and owls are on show. You can see one of the frequent displays of free-flying by eagles, vultures and kites and watch cormorants dive with pinpoint accuracy into a glass-sided pool in pursuit of eels. (The park, 3km north-west of La Faute, takes its name from the hamlet nearby rather than from any connection with the USA.) ⧺ 1 Mar-1 Oct, daily 10am-noon & 2-6pm (1 Apr-16 Sept, daily 9.30am-noon & 2-7pm). Route de La Tranche-sur-Mer (tel : 51 27 10 48). 35F.

Aqua-Vendée. Guided tours, in French, of an establishment raising 1.5 million eels followed by tastings of the product (smoked), washed down with a glass of local wine. You need to make up a group of at least 10 people, and book in advance. ■ Chemin des Pensées, La Faute-sur-Mer (tel : 51 27 17 41). 25F.

LONGEVILLE-SUR-MER

Village 25km west of Luçon, and stranded a couple of kilometres from the sea, beyond a forest of pines and holm oaks.
Market : Friday.
Festival : Foire à la Brocante (antiques fair), mid-July and mid-August.
La Pierre qui Vire. Unless a farmer has thoughtlessly surrounded it with a maize crop, this large standing-stone, also known as the Menhir du Russelet, can be seen on the skyline amid open fields about 1km west of the village. To reach it, turn south at the hamlet of La Raisinière. The menhir has had so many other large stones dumped around it, that it is hard to credit the local legend which says that it spins around each day at midnight. ■

LUÇON

The rather garish light-industrial sprawl around its fringes gives a false impression of this attractive town at the junction of the plain with the Vendée's southern marshes. Artfully-trained and pollarded trees form green arches in summer above the roads that lead to the centre, which is dominated as much by a crazily-decorated concrete water-tower north of the Champ-de-Foire (built to commemorate the garrisoning of a regiment of dragoons in the town) as by the elegant 85m spire of the cathedral. Although Luçon suffered a great deal at the hands of the Huguenots during the War of Religion it escaped relatively unscathed from the later Wars of the Vendée since it was a Republican stronghold. The streets - notably Rue de l'Hôtel-de-Ville - are lined with substantial two-storey houses of solid white stone and organised into an incredibly complicated one-way system. The town's main shopping areas are Rue Georges-Clemenceau and Rue du Président-de-Gaulle ; the market is behind the cathedral, off Rue Victor Hugo.
Market : Wednesday and Saturday.
Specialities : Liqueurs.
Brocante : Dépôt-Vente de la Vendée, Les Quatre Chemins (on D949, 5km east of Luçon), Ste-Gemme-la-Plaine. Thurs-Mon 2-7pm (closed public holidays).
Cathedral. Richelieu, who was bishop here from 1606 to 1622, said Mass beneath its graceful spire and soaring white columns. Carved Romanesque faces of humans and animals are seen alongside 17th-century stone garlands in a mixture of architectural styles that range from the 12th to the 18th centuries. The church is linked to the bishops' palace by beautifully-preserved 16th-century cloisters. Concerts are sometimes given on the monumental organ, presented to the city of Luçon by the Emperor Napoléon III. ■
Jardin Dumaine. Large garden in the town centre where you can wander among gravel paths, formal borders, collections of interesting trees and shrubs and a

impressive avenues of 150-year-old yew hedges towering almost 7m high. There is a charming Victorian-style bandstand for summer concerts, and children are bound to love the topiary animals that recall the fables of La Fontaine - mostly familiar to British children, since the 17th-century French writer cribbed them from Aesop. ▪ Daily 7.30am-7pm (1 Apr-30 Sept, daily 7.30am-9pm). Access via Rue de l'Hôtel-de-Ville or Allée St-François. Free.

H. Vrignaud Fils. Opposite the cathedral is the former distillery (the new one is located outside the town) of a company that manufactures a coffee-based liqueur called Kamok. You can drop into this delightfully old-fashioned, wood-floored shop for a "dégustation" (tasting) of this and some of Vrignaud's other specialities - including Liqueur des Vendéens, a marriage of orange and brandy. ▪ Tues-Sat 9am-noon & 2.30-7pm. 1 Place Richelieu (tel : 51 56 11 48).

Lac des Guifettes. In summer you can enjoy swimming, tennis, archery, mini-golf and watersports on a 42-hectare lake, 2km south of the town. ▪

MAILLEZAIS

Village on the edge of the Venise Verte, 30km east of Luçon, above which tower the ruins of its ancient monastical buildings (see below).

Traditional craft, and also canoes, may be hired to cruise the canals of the Venise Verte (see page 69) between Easter and late September. Reckon on around 85F per 5-person boat to be paddled by a guide for a 45-minute trip ; 110F for two hours under your own steam.

Market : Sunday in July and August at Maillé, 6km south-west of Maillezais.

Specialities : Préfou, a type of garlic bread ; Jams, purées, syrups and fruit products from J-J. Aubert, Récolte de Petits Fruits, Liez, 2.5km east of Maillezais.

Abbaye St-Pierre. Just west of the village rise the magnificent, ghostly remains of an early 11th-century abbey, a dazzling example of Romanesque architecture. Some 200 monks lived here in the 13th century, undertaking the first draining of the area to create the productive fields that exist today. A century later, the writer Rabelais (see Fontenay-le-Comte, page 73) spent three years within its walls. After the Revolution the abbey was confiscated by the state and sold for demolition. In the former kitchen of the monastery a "musée lapidaire" (stone museum) allows you a closer look at some of the detailed Romanesque carvings. Occasional concerts and son-et-lumière performances are given in summer. ▪ Fri-Wed 9am-12.30pm & 2-6pm, Thurs 2-6pm (1 June-31 Aug, daily 9am-8pm). 12F, children 7F50.

MAREUIL-SUR-LAY

Picturesque wine-producing town overlooking the river Lay, 9.5km north-west of Luçon, dominated by the spire of its austere Romanesque church and a beautiful but dilapidated 16th-century castle. A signposted Route des Vins leads to some of the many vineyards on the outskirts of the town and around the tiny village of Rosnay, 5km to the west, which claims the highest wine output per head of population in France - almost 10 per cent of its 452 inhabitants are wine producers. A list of growers offering "dégustations" (tastings) is available from local tourist offices. Fishing in the river Lay and in the Lac du Château-Guibert, 3km to the north ; signposted walks along the river.

Market : Thursday.

Speciality : Fiefs Vendéens wine.

Pont de Lavaud. The great French engineer Gustave Eiffel (1832-1923) designed this simple iron bridge, 4km south-west of Mareuil, in 1866 to carry country traffic on chunky stone pillars across the river Lay. ▪

Parachute memorial. A granite monument on the D50, just to the west of Eiffel's bridge (see above), commemorates the first parachute drop of arms to Vendean Resistance workers on 14 July 1943. Once they picked up the poetical coded message "Pourquoi me réveiller au souffle du printemps ?" (Why awaken me at the first breath of spring ?) via the BBC in London, they prepared to retrieve the precious consignment which they hid in the house beside the monument. ▪

LE POIRÉ-SUR-VELLUIRE

A village on the edge of a 250-hectare reserve, 21km east of Luçon, that is being run experimentally on a system of "commons". After the winter (during which the land is often completely submerged under water), the locals have the right to turn their horses, cows and geese out to graze - a springtime event which is celebrated with a colourful festival. The area is visited by migrating birds (including the occasional pair of storks) which you can view from an observatory.

Festival : Opening of the village for new season's grazing rights, late April.
Speciality : Wines from the village of Vix, 6km to the south-east.

ILE DE RÉ (Charente-Maritime)

A dramatically curving bridge, almost 3km in length, links the 26km-long island with La Pallice, just north of La Rochelle - the toll payable for a car is around 60F return, rising from June to September (a period when the Ile de Ré is uncomfortably crowded) to more than 100F You can rent bicycles to explore the sandy coast or to follow signposted routes along lanes bordered by low, whitewashed cottages with brightly-painted shutters, their gardens studded with tall hollyhocks. The "paludiers" or salt producers still work their rectangular salt-pans from which the hot sun evaporates the sea-water, leaving behind a white deposit to be raked into little pyramids and eventually sold as "fleur de sel". The island's donkeys were at one time dressed in checked trousers and straw hats to protect them from sun and insects while they worked in marshes and seaside fields, though today you will find them only on postcards.

Specialities : Sea salt, asparagus & early vegetables, oysters, wine, Pineau-des Charentes (fortified wine drunk as an apéritif).

St-Martin-de-Ré. The island's capital, on the north coast, has quaint narrow, cobble streets. The extensive fortifications date back to the 17th century, after the town wa besieged by the English.

LA ROCHELLE (Charente-Maritime)

This large town, with a strikingly attractive central area clustered round the pictu resque Vieux-Port, is one of France's yachting capitals. Two large towers - the Tou St-Nicolas and the Tour de la Chaîne - guard the harbour entrance, and in the marin hundreds of streamlined craft float at their moorings.

In the 16th century the town was fiercely Protestant and thus was bloodily involve in the Wars of Religion. The city successfully resisted a long siege by the Duke c Anjou in 1573 ; a subsequent one (1627-28) led by Cardinal Richelieu left only 5,0C survivors from a population of 28,000. Later inhabitants became prosperous on t proceeds of the highly lucrative West Indian sugar and slave trades.

If you take a stroll through the streets that surround the Hôtel de Ville (town hall) be sure to take in the 16th-century Maison Henri II, the mirrored gilt splendour of the Café de la Paix on Rue Chaudrier, the old arcades that line Rue du Minage, the half-timbered buildings in Grande-Rue des Merciers, the fairy-tale-style town hall itself, and the Porte de la Grosse Horloge that was formerly the gateway between port and city. Principal shopping areas are neatly contained within Grande-Rue des Merciers and Rue du Palais, the east and west boundaries of the old town.

You can take a short boat trip by "bus de mer" (waterbus) from the old port to the new marina and beach at Les Minimes, and longer ones, with commentary about the town's history, from the north side of the old port. The tourist office organises tours of the old town on foot and by horse-drawn carriage.

Markets : Daily, Place du Marché ; Sunday, La Pallice, 2km west of the town centre.

Arts and Crafts : 15 June-15 Sept, daily, near the towers.

Brocante : Foire de la Brocante (antiques fair) end-April/early May ; Marché aux Puces (flea market), Saturday, Rue St-Nicolas (1 July-31 Aug, Thursday & Saturday) ; Salon des Antiquaires (antiques fair), mid-November.

Festivals : Carnival, mid-May ; Film festival, late June/early July ; Francofolies (festival of popular music and culture), mid-July ; Le Grand Pavois (in-water boat show), mid-September.

Specialities : Charentais melons, chaudrée (fish soup with white wine), mouclade (mussels in cream sauce), Pineau-des-Charentes (a fortified wine drunk, chilled, as an apéritif).

Tour St-Nicolas. The largest of the three imposing towers that dominate the harbour, standing to the east of the entrance. On show inside are models and plans showing the port's history. ■ Wed-Mon 9.30am-12.30pm & 2-5pm (1 Apr-30 Sept, Wed-Mon 9.30am-12.30pm & 2-6.30pm ; 1 June-31 Aug, daily 9.30am-7pm). Tel : 46 41 74 13. 20F, children 6F.

Tour de la Chaine. Across the harbour mouth, a second 14th-century tower contains a relief map of the city as it was before the siege, explained with the aid of a mini "son-et-lumière" show. ⊭ Palm Sunday-30 Apr, daily 2-6.30pm ; 1 May-30 Sept, daily 9.30am-noon & 2-6.30pm ; 1 Oct-11 Nov, Sat, Sun 2-6pm. Tel : 46 50 52 36. 15F, children 8F.

Tour de la Lanterne. A little farther west than the other two towers, this former lighthouse and prison contains some amazing graffiti inscribed by 17th- and 18th-century captives, many of them English sailors who carved images of the ships in which they had served on to the soft stone walls of their jail. ■ Wed-Mon 9.30am-12.30pm & 2-5pm (1 Apr-30 Sept, Wed-Mon 9.30am-12.30pm & 2-6.30pm ; 1 June-31 Aug, daily 9.30am-7pm). Tel : 46 41 56 04. 20F, children 6F.

Aquarium. Fish from all over the world swim past in Atlantic, Mediterranean and tropical tanks (you can have the sensation of joining them when you pass through a 7m glass tunnel). Sharks and other larger creatures cruise around a vast tank where you can watch (and talk to) divers carrying out maintenance and feeding. ■ Daily 10am-noon & 2-7pm (1-30 June, daily 9am-7pm ; 1 July-31 Aug, daily 9am-11pm). Port des Minimes (tel : 46 44 00 00). 39F, children 20F.

Musée Grevin. La Rochelle's answer to Madame Tussaud's. Waxwork figures convey the history of the town through 15 scenes, from its founding in 1199 by Eleanor of Aquitaine, through siege and slave trade, to the deportation and execution of a 79-year-old mayor in 1944. ■ Daily 9am-9pm (1 June-30 Sept, daily 9am-11pm). 38

Cours des Dames (tel : 46 41 08 71). 27F, children 18F.

Musée Rochelais de la Dernière Guerre. Photographs, posters, uniforms and objects relating to the German occupation of the town during the Second World War, displayed in an old wartime bunker. * 1 July-31 Aug, Tues-Sat 10am-6pm. 8 Rue des Dames (tel : 46 34 02 67). 22F, children 18F.

Musée du Flacon à Parfum. More than 1,000 perfume bottles from nine countries in this charming and unusual collection near the Grosse Horloge. ▪ Mon 2-7pm, Tues-Sat 10am-noon & 2-7pm (1 July-31 Aug, Mon 2-7pm, Tues-Sat 10am-noon & 2-7pm, Sun & public holidays 2-6pm). 33 Rue du Temple (tel : 46 41 32 40). 20F, children 15F.

Musée du Nouveau Monde. Paintings, drawings, sculptures and maps tell the story of the town's links with the New World - America, Canada and, in particular, the West Indies - through emigration, plantation-owning and the slave trade. The museum is housed in a grand 18th-century mansion. ▪ Wed-Mon 10.30am-12.30pm & 1.30-6pm, Sun 3-6pm. 10 Rue Fleuriau (tel : 46 41 46 50). 12F, children 10F.

ST-CYR-EN-TALMONDAIS

Small village 12km west of Luçon, at the junction of the bocage and the marshes.

Court d'Aron. A magnificent floral park spread over more than 10 hectares, featuring lakes covered in exquisite pink lotus flowers, plus woodland walks and green lawns. The 17th-century-style mansion, embellished with turrets, that stands on the edge of the gardens is open during the summer months for you to admire its monumental period fireplaces, and collections of Flemish and Gobelins tapestries, paintings, porcelain and sculpture. Park ⌗ 1 Apr-30 Sept, daily 10am-7pm. 30F, children 14F ; House * 1 July-31 Aug, half-hour guided tours daily 10am-noon & 2-6pm. 9F, children 6F (plus admission to park).

ST-DENIS-DU-PAYRÉ

Small village 13km south-west of Luçon.
Festival : Foire aux célibataires (singles festival), early August.

Réserve Naturelle Michel-Brosselin. Depending on the time of year you can peer through telescopes set up in the observatory of this 200-hectare wildlife reserve, lying just to the east of the village, at such resident birds as ducks, harriers and egrets, or more unusual migratory visitors like storks. ⌗ 1 Feb-30 June, first Sun of month 2.30-6pm ; 1 July-31 Aug, daily 10am-noon & 3-7pm. Tel : 51 27 23 92. 17F.

STE-HERMINE

Village on the edge of the plain, 12km north-east of Luçon, in the centre of which stands a monumental First World War memorial featuring the politician George Clemenceau (see Jard-sur-Mer, page 49, Mouilleron-en-Pareds, page 76 and Mou champs, page 91) and several "Poilus" - the affectionate nickname for French soldier of 1914-18. There is an interesting turn-of-the-century market hall, built in the sty of Victor Baltard, who was responsible for the 19th-century markets of Paris.
Market : Friday.

ST-MICHEL-EN-L'HERM

This former island of whitewashed houses, 15km south-west of Luçon, seems hig when seen across the open marshland of the Marais Poitevin, though it rises on

17m above sea level. Just to the north, as you drive along the Triaize road, you can glimpse a strange feature at the hamlet of Les Chaux - the remains of some enormous banks of oyster shells, several feet high (the farmhouse itself has been built on one of them). No one knows the origin, but they date back for many centuries and are thought to have been fortifications against the sea (which used to lap against this village) or protection from invading Normans.

Market : Thursday.

Specialities : Eels, cheese (Petit-Vendéen, La Micheline).

Abbey ruins. The remains of a Benedictine abbey, first established in the 7th century, but reconstructed several times since owing to the Hundred Years' War, the onslaught of the Protestants in the Wars of Religion, and finally the Wars of the Vendée. The parts that are still intact include the vaulted 17th-century chapter-house and the refectory. The monks were among those who undertook the draining of the marshes that formed the flat landscape of fields that surround the village today (see Chaillé-les-Marais, page 61). * 1 July-31 Aug, guided tours Tues, Thurs & Fri 10am-noon & 3-5pm. Tel : 51 30 21 89. 10F

LA TRANCHE-SUR-MER

The other facet of this popular seaside resort and windsurfers' paradise, 32km south-west of Luçon, is a great, though comparatively recent, floral tradition (see below) that dates from 1953 when a couple of Dutch bulb-growers opened the eyes of the townspeople to the idea of using their sandy soil to start a bulb industry.

Boats run to La Rochelle and the Ile de Ré with Croisières Inter-Iles et Fluviales (tel : 51 30 33 39).

Markets : Tuesday and Saturday, Place de la Libération ; Wednesday, La Grière car park.

Festival : Parade of flowers, late April.

Specialities : Flowering bulbs, garlic, onions.

Floralies. Bulb fields and woodland walks are ablaze with colour and dramatic, formal patterns : crocuses, narcissi and tulips bloom in spring ; begonias, petunias, gladioli and carnations through the summer months. ⧣ 1 Mar-30 Apr & 1 July-30 Sept, daily 10am-7pm. Boulevard de la Petite-Hollande (tel : 51 30 33 96). 22F, children 12F, disabled free.

TRIAIZE

Attractive marshland village, 7.5km south of Luçon, grouped around a restored 12th-century church with an unusual spire that looks something like a partially-inflated, wavy sausage-balloon. The village has perpetuated the once-widespread custom of making "bouses", dung-pats that could be burnt to serve for cooking and for heating even the ash made a valuable fertiliser. At the annual festival the fuel is put to good use for cooking eels, mussels, mogettes and other regional specialities.

Festival : Fête de la Bouse (cowpat festival), late July.

LA VENISE VERTE

This labyrinth of tranquil, duckweed-covered canals edged with poplars and willows, known as "Green Venice" is one of the Vendée's most entrancing features and by far the prettiest corner of the vast marshland known as the Marais Poitevin. You can rent a workaday "plate" (flat-bottomed boat) - with or without a guide to paddle it (English-speaking ones can be booked in advance) - from several villages in the area :

Maillezais, Le Mazeau, Damvix, La Garette and, most attractive of all, Coulon (see page 62). Since you can fit six or seven people into one boat, the hourly hire fee of from about 125F (85F if you forgo the guide) is quite a bargain. Lifejackets are nowhere to be seen, so take your own if you worry about small children going overboard, though the canals are so shallow that you could probably fish them out before too much harm was done. Some companies own picnic sites where their clients can moor to enjoy lunch in one of the green fields along the banks - ask before you decide which firm is to enjoy your custom.

The maze of tiny "rigoles", or canals, that run into the Sèvre Niortaise river were created first by monks in the 12th and 13th centuries, and completed by Dutch engineers 500 years later. The tree-lined waterways, which serve partly as drainage for the pastures and partly as avenues of transport for everything from wedding parties to cattle, are blissfully silent, except for the buzz of dragonflies and the giggles of incompetent crews zigzagging inelegantly from bank to bank (the locals glide effortlessly past with the merest flick of their paddles).

As well as freshwater fish and eels, the still, green waters shelter colonies of otters - becoming as rare in France as they are in England - and attract hundreds of glittering dragonflies.

Landlubbers can explore the area on foot or rent bikes from Arçais, 9km south-west of Coulon, from where there are signposted cycle routes of 10, 15 and 40km - and no many hills ! For the really lazy summer visitor there are two other ways to tour : a little train-like vehicle called Pibalou (tel : 49 35 02 29) which makes several trips a day between Coulon and Le Mazeau, 10km to the west ; or the Grenouillon minibu (tel : 49 35 08 08) which offers two-hour jaunts from Coulon.

Specialities : Eels, "lumas" (snails), "coulonnais" (light, fluffy cakes), and lamb with mogettes.

CHAPTER 4

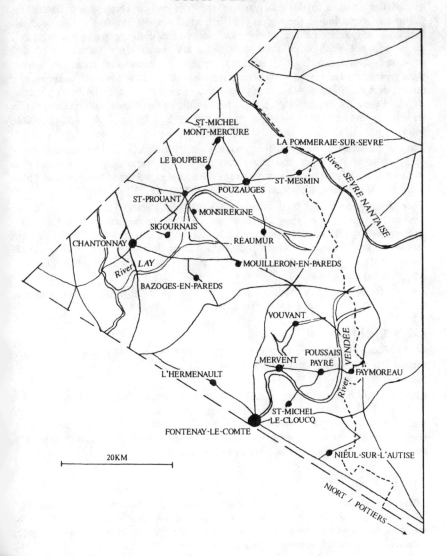

ST-MICHEL MONT-MERCURE

LA POMMERAIE-SUR-SEVRE

LE BOUPERE

ST-MESMIN

POUZAUGES

River SEVRE NANTAISE

ST-PROUANT

MONSIREIGNE

SIGOURNAIS

CHANTONNAY

RÉAUMUR

River LAY

MOUILLERON-EN-PAREDS

BAZOGES-EN-PAREDS

VOUVANT

VENDÉE

MERVENT

FOUSSAIS PAYRÉ

FAYMOREAU

L'HERMENAULT

River

ST-MICHEL-LE-CLOUCQ

FONTENAY-LE-COMTE

20KM

NIÉUL-SUR-L'AUTISE

NIORT / POITIERS

BAZOGES-EN-PAREDS

As you drive across the rolling green hills of the bocage, you can easily spot this village, 12km south-east of Chantonnay, by its huge castle keep crowned by a distinctive, pointed watch-tower. Bazoges is a beautiful place, managing to purvey an old-world atmosphere, yet with a pleasantly un-fossilised look. Solid stone buildings look on to the square that surrounds the fortified stronghold and the ancient church.
Festival : Foire aux marrons (chestnut festival with local food specialities, craft stalls and brocante), late October at La Caillère-St-Hilaire, 3km south of Bazoges.

Musée d'Arts et Traditions Populaires. Guided tours of the excellent museum, in one of the cottages in the courtyard of the "donjon" or keep, give a fascinating glimpse of rural life in the region (you can ask for a descriptive sheet in English). Evocative images are painted of the rural way of life until comparatively recently : people did not wash more than their faces and hands since they believed dirt prevented disease entering through empty pores and babies that could crawl were tightly swaddled and placed upright with their legs in a hollow container to keep them out of danger. A huge 14th-century dovecote, which could contain 3,000 pigeons, stands at the back overlooking an area that is soon to be planted with medieval-style fruit-trees, herbs and other horticultural features. ▪ Sun 2-6pm (1 Apr-15 Sept, Wed-Mon 2-6pm). Tel : 51 51 25 19. 15F, children 10F.

Donjon. Restoration work is still in progress on the magnificent 12th-century tower that dominates the town. You can climb the narrow spiral stairs for a wonderful panoramic view from the gallery that runs round the entire top of the building. ▪ Sun 2-6pm (1 Apr-15 Sept, Wed-Mon 2-6pm). Tel : 51 51 25 19. 10F, children 5F.

Ciste des Cous. Off the road, about 1km south-west towards La Jaudonnière, is an unusual, circular, stone-flagged, now roofless enclosure dating from 3000BC. Excavations in 1913 revealed more than 100 skeletons that had been placed in this prehistoric burial chamber, which you can still enter through a low tunnel. Some of the finds are displayed in the Abbaye de Ste-Croix museum at Les Sables-d'Olonne (see page 56). ▪

Lac de Rochereau. Man-made lake, 5km north-west of the village, where you can walk, picnic and, in summer, sail, canoe, windsurf and fish. ▪

LE BOUPERE

Pretty hilltop village, 8km west of Pouzauges, with streets tightly clustered about its central feature, the 12th-century church (see below).
Market : Tuesday.

Church. This curious building looks, from some angles, more like a castle. Its imposing fortifications - including loopholes, machicolations (through which stones and other unwelcoming objects were dropped on attackers) and a stone gallery running around the top - were added three centuries after its construction to protect church and villagers during the Wars of Religion. ▪

CHANTONNAY

Attractive market town in the centre of the Vendée, 21km from Pouzauges, known as "the gateway to the bocage" for its position on the edge of the landscape of woods and hills that stretches away to the north-east. Just to the south of the town is Pont-Charrault (sometimes written Pont-Charron), a bridge over the Grand Lay river that was the site of one of the first resounding victories for the Vendeans over the Republican forces in 1793.
Market : Tuesday, Thursday and Saturday.

Lakes. You can swim or fish in the Lac du Moulin-Neuf, 6km south of Chantonnay on the river Lay, follow a signposted walk around the edge or, in summer, try your hand at archery as well as sailing, canoeing and windsurfing.
Sailing, fishing, walking, pedaloes and picnics can be enjoyed on and around the Lac de Rochereau about 6km to the east of the town (see above). ▪

FAYMOREAU-LES-MINES

Village on the eastern border of the Vendée, 16km north-east of Fontenay-le-Comte, in an area rich with memories of the French industrial revolution. Coal was mined in the region from the late 18th century until 1958. A few relics remain, like the pit-head tower at Èpagne, 3km east of Vouvant.

Maison de la Mine et des Mineurs. The history of the local mining industry is told through audio-visual devices and displays of tools and documents inside one of the first miner's houses to be built in the village of La Verrerie, 2km north-west of Faymoreau. Maps are available to guide you past mines and other industrial relics like glassworks and a disused, coal-fired power station. ♯ 1 Apr-30 Sept, Sun & public holidays 3-7pm (1 July-31 Aug, Wed-Mon 3-7pm. La Verrerie (tel : 51 00 42 66). 8F, children 4F

FONTENAY-LE-COMTE

Ancient streets lined with Renaissance houses - once the haunt of poets, scientists, philosophers and lawyers - indicate the former importance of a place that, until the French Revolution of 1789, was the capital of the Bas-Poitou (as the Vendée was known until that time). The town, lying near the south-eastern corner of the département at the junction of the plain and the steep, wooded hills of the bocage, was razed to the ground by the English and later, having a strong Protestant population, knew considerable turmoil during the Wars of Religion.

The writer-monk François Rabelais (c1495-1553) - creator of two legendary giants of French literature - spent almost 16 years in the town as a Benedictine monk, before removing to the abbey of Maillezais in 1524. In a series of satiric allegories that sparkle with bawdy vitality, the Renaissance humorist told of Gargantua, who rode on a mare as big as six elephants, and of his son, Pantagruel, who shattered the mighty ship's chains that bound him into his cradle with one blow of his infant fist, who learnt all knowledge and all languages, and who once sheltered a whole army from the rain beneath his tongue. (Elsewhere on the scale of literature, the novelist Georges Simenon - who lived here during the Second World War - used the town as a backdrop for the adventures of his fictional detective in "Maigret a Peur", where a serial killer haunts its uncharacteristically rain-sodden streets.)

The status of Fontenay was overturned after the Vendée wars when Napoleon deemed it be too far from the geographical centre of the département to quell any new peasant uprisings, and picked on the then small village of La Roche-sur-Yon as his new capital.

The town is laid out on both sides of the Vendée river. At the top is the leafy square known as Place Viète (named after the 16th-century mathematician, born in Fontenay, who is credited with the creation of modern algebra from the ancient form invented in Babylon, Egypt and India). This side of the river buzzes with activity on Saturday mornings, when the market is in full swing and the stalls fill the streets - the food-hall is by the bank of the river, not far from arcaded Place Belliard and Rue du Pont-aux-Chèvres, both lined with interesting old houses. The elegantly-sculpted 16th-century Fontaine des Quatre-Tias, from which the name "Fontenay" derives, is little to the north of the market-hall. On the eastern side of the river, across the Pont aux Sardines, you can stroll along the pedestrianised Rue des Loges which has kept the picturesque shop-fronts and ancient houses of stone or half-timbering from the days when it was the town's main street.

The tourist office, located in a small, free-standing tower by the river, can arrange guided tours on foot or by horse-drawn carriage, a 20-minute pleasure flight over the town and the nearby forest of Mervent-Vouvant in July and August, or even some lessons at Fontenay's thriving croquet club - venue for the 1995 World Croquet Championships.

Market : Saturday.

Specialities : Fiefs Vendéens wines from Pissotte, 4km north of the town.

Musée Vendéen. You should really come here to get a feel for the town's history before walking around its streets. Prehistoric remains and gallo-roman glass, found locally during archaeological digs ; 19th-century furniture ; the bird life of the region ; and furniture typical of the southern Vendée. The second floor contains works by local artists like Paul Baudry (see La Roche-sur-Yon, page 55), Charles Milcendeau (see Soullans, page 41) and wood-engraver and etcher Auguste Lepère (1849-1918), and a model of the town's old quarters, complete with sound effects. Acoustiguide available in English. ▪ Wed-Sun 2-6pm (16 June-15 Sept, Wed-Fri 2-6pm ; Sat, Sun & public holidays 10am-noon & 2-6pm). Rue du 137e RI, near Place Viète & Notre-Dame church (tel : 51 69 31 31). 11F

Château de Terre-Neuve. Nicolas Rapin, a 16th-century poet and magistrate of Fontenay, created this exquisite, fairy-tale-style stately home which he adorned with pinnacles, turrets and mullioned windows. Terracotta statues of the Muses look down from the façade. Today it is a private home, but visitors are given 45-minute guided tours of some of the beautifully-furnished rooms. You are shown two magnificent fireplaces - one showing the search for the "philosopher's stone" (that alchemists believed would turn base metals into gold), and the other decorated with griffons - and mellow wooden panelling from the château of Chambord, in the Loire valley, plus collections of keys, ivory, costumes and Old Master paintings. A section is devoted to the etching plates of Octave de Rochebrune, the artist who was responsible for restoring the château in the 19th century. ♯ 1-31 May, daily 2-6pm ; 1 June-30 Sept, daily 9am-noon & 2-7pm. Tel : 51 69 99 41 or 51 69 17 75. 18F, children 11F

Église Notre-Dame. The church's slender 15th-century spire, reaching 82.5 metres into the sky, can be seen from almost everywhere in town. A 1,000-year-old crypt lies beneath, its vaulted ceiling held up by Byzantine-style pillars. For a bird's-eye view of the town, you can climb the tower (enquire at the museum next door). ▪

FOUSSAIS-PAYRÉ

This picturesque village, 16km north-east of Fontenay-le-Comte, is renowned for its ancient church, its Renaissance houses (some half-timbered), and its 17th-century market-hall. L'Auberge Ste-Catherine (St Catherine's Inn) was formerly the family home of François Viète (1540-1603), the French mathematician (see Fontenay-le-Comte, page 73).

Market : Wednesday in July and August.

Riding : Manoir de Vux, Foussais-Payré (tel : 51 51 43 93). Rides in the Mervent Vouvant forest, horse-drawn wagon trips, hostel accommodation and meals.

Romanesque church. Admirers come from afar to marvel at the sculpted façade of this 11th-century church. Although the wall has had to be reinforced with buttresses these have been ingeniously designed not to obscure the beautifully carved panel either side of the doorway that show a Crucifixion scene and the risen Christ with the disciples at Emmaus. Over the doorway you can make out weird animals, and the figure of Christ between the symbols of the four Evangelists. Concerts are often held in the church in summer. ▪

74

L'HERMENAULT

Large village, 12km north-west of Fontenay-le-Comte, with ramparts and several attractive old houses.

Market : Wednesday.

Festivals : "48 Heures du Chien" (a two-day event involving more than 20,000 animals, beginning with a sale of dogs and horses on the Saturday, followed by a dog show on the Sunday), late August at Marsais-Ste-Radégonde, 3km north of L'Hermenault ; Fête du Tabac et des Produits du Terroir (Festival of tobacco and of local produce), early August at St-Martin-des-Fontaines, 3.5km north of the village.

Château de L'Hermenault. For a few weeks of summer you can visit the grounds surrounding the remains of a 14th-century castle that was once the summer residence of the bishops of La Rochelle. The writer Rabelais (see Fontenay-le-Comte, page 73) was a frequent guest, and wrote of having given some plane trees to his hosts - certainly some very old ones spread their branches above the pasture-land. The building was much damaged after the Revolution, when it was confiscated and sold. Inside one of the outbuildings, a fine barn, the woodwork of the roof resembles that of an inverted boat. * 1 July-15 Aug, daily 2-5pm. Rue du Château. Free.

MERVENT

Hillside village in the heart of the vast Mervent-Vouvant forest, 7km north of Fontenay-le-Comte. In the summer the area is popular with holidaymakers who come to enjoy the swimming, windsurfing, canoeing and pedalo trips on the lake that lies at the lower end of the village, created by dams across the Mère and Vendée rivers. Signposted walks lead through 2,400 hectares of oaks and chestnuts - especially beautiful in autumn - that are still home to deer and wild boar. Climbers can practise their skills on the rocks of Pierre-Blanche.

Specialities : Fiefs Vendéens wines from Pissotte, 5km south-west of the village.

Zoo de Mervent. Some 350 animals live in large enclosures on wooded slopes at the edge of the forest, 3km south-east of the village. The natural lifestyles and habitats of the birds, reptiles, monkeys, big cats and other creatures are explained in detail. ■ Daily 9am-7pm. Gros Roc (tel : 51 00 22 54). 36F, children 18F.

Parc de Pierre-Brune. Large leisure park in a forest setting 2km north of Mervent. Bouncy castles, adventure playground, train-rides, mini-golf, bumper-boats and mini-karting - enough to keep the children amused for hours. ♯ Easter-31 Oct, daily 2-7pm (1 June-31 Aug, daily 10am-8pm). Tel : 51 00 25 53. 20F.

Grotte du Père Montfort. Candles burn in this little cave halfway-down a precipitous, rocky slope in the forest, overlooking the river Mère opposite Pierre-Brune and about 3km north-west of Mervent village. Follow the red marks painted on the rocks to discover this shrine where Louis-Marie Grignion de Montfort lived for a time in about 1715, during a mission to convert the region's many Protestants to Catholicism. He is commemorated in St-Laurent-sur-Sèvre (see page 92) where he founded several religious orders. The cave is signposted to the east off the D938ter, but you can also approach it from below, near the Pierre-Brune dam. ■

Maison des Amis de la Forêt. Stuffed animals, videos, and displays of mushrooms, tools and wooden objects show life in the forest and the uses made of the wood and other materials harvested there. The museum overlooks the lake, some 2km northeast of the village. Children love the adventure playground with its dare-devil "deathslide" and other wood-built amusements. There is also a mini-golf with 18 holes, each one designed to represent a different local tourist attraction, plus a bar and a cut-price general store. ♯ Easter-31 Oct, Mon-Fri 9am-noon & 2-5.30pm, Sun 2-5.30pm. La Jamonière (tel : 51 00 27 26). 10F, children 7F

Château de la Citardière. About 2km north-east of Mervent stands a curiously solid, moated Renaissance castle the top of which is decorated with impressive stone spouts that look like cannons. You can go inside one or two of its vaulted rooms or enjoy an afternoon snack at the crêperie on the ground floor (open Fri, Sat 5-9pm, Sun noon-9pm). Concerts and other cultural events take place in the summer months. ♯ 15 June-15 Sept. Tel : 51 00 27 04.

MONSIREIGNE

Village perched on a hilltop overlooking the green valleys of the bocage, 10km south-west of Pouzauges.

Musée de la France Protestante de l'Ouest. This museum, in a country house 3km north-east of the village, explains four centuries of Protestantism in western France through photographs, documents, and such objects as the tokens worn by clandestine worshippers during the times of intolerance.

Jean Calvin (1509-64), the French Reformist, spent some time spreading his doctrine in Poitiers in 1534 and western France acquired a strong Huguenot (as Calvin's brand of Protestantism became known) tradition, particularly the town of Fontenay-le-Comte. The Wars of Religion (1562-98) pitched Catholics against Protestants, causing death and the destruction of religious buildings on a grand scale. Eventually Henri IV (who had been himself a Protestant) converted to Catholicism on his accession to the French throne in 1589, and nine years later issued the Edict of Nantes which brought the long religious struggle to an end. This law allowed Protestants freedom of worship, and endured for almost a century until Louis XIV revoked it, causing more than 400,000 Huguenots to flee overseas (many to Britain). Only with the Revolution in 1789 were their political and civil rights restored.

Many Protestants still live in this area - you will see in St-Prouant, Mouilleron-en-Pareds and other villages, streets named Rue du Temple (after the name given to an "église réformée" or French Protestant church). * 1 July-15 Sept, Tues-Sat 11am-7pm. Le Bois-Tiffrais (tel : 51 57 24 39). 12F, children 8F

MOUILLERON-EN-PAREDS

Unspoilt town, 16km east of Chantonnay, that was the birthplace of not just one, but two of France's most famous wartime leaders : Georges Clemenceau (1841-1929) and Jean de Lattre de Tassigny (1889-1952). If you are within earshot of the Romanesque church just before the hour strikes, you can hear a carillon of 13 bells play "Ave Maria" before the chimes. (It probably doesn't seem so attractive if you have to listen to it 24 times a day.)

Maison Natale de Jean de Lattre. Delightful, cosy, bourgeois house built in the 1860s, home of the maternal grandparents of Jean de Lattre. The distinguished French soldier was decorated eight times in the First World War, became a general at the start of the Second World War, then commander of the French First Army that landed in Provence in January 1944, liberated Alsace and crossed the Rhine and the Danube rivers, and accepted the surrender of Germany on 8 May 1945. The three floors of the house are filled with family furniture and mementoes, and details of the Marshal's career, including his later service as commander-in-chief of the French forces in Indochina in the early 1950s. Part of the display is devoted to his only son who was killed in Indochina in 1951 and who lies buried beside his father in the town's cemetery - their graves marked with simple white crosses. ■ Wed-Mon, 10am-noon & 2-5pm (15 Apr-15 Oct, Wed-Mon 9.30am-noon & 2-6pm). Rue de Lattre (tel : 51 00 31 49). 17F, children free.

Musée National des Deux Victoires. Personal relics, photographs, films and documents relating to the signing by Georges Clemenceau of the Treaty of Versailles, at the end of the First World War, alongside objects, papers and photographs concerning Jean de Lattre's signature in Berlin on behalf of France at the conclusion of the Second World War. ■ Wed-Mon 10am-noon & 2-5pm (15 Apr-15 Oct, 9.30am-noon & 2-6pm). Opposite the Mairie (tel : 51 00 31 49). 17F, children free.

Rochers de Mouilleron. On the eastern edge of the town, starting from the ancient pump and washing-place, you can take the Sentier des Meuniers (the Millers' Path) once a busy thoroughfare for donkeys and ponies carrying bags of corn and flour. Splashes of yellow paint underfoot lead you up past trees and rocks to a windy ridge where you find three majestic windmills (of which one is now an oratory to the remembrance of Maréchal de Lattre de Tassigny). Like those on the Mont des Alouettes (see page 88) these mills and the other 11 that once stood beside them played an important signalling role in the Wars of the Vendée. ■

BALLIER MICHAËL

NIEUL-SUR-L'AUTISE

Eleanor of Aquitaine, queen of France through her first marriage to Louis VII and later queen of England after becoming the wife of Henry Plantagenet, is said to have been born at her father's castle here, 10km south-east of Fontenay-le-Comte. The group of monastic buildings in the heart of the village (see below) is the most intact set to survive in the whole of Poitou.

Festival : Fête de la Meunerie (milling festival), Whitsun weekend in odd-numbered years.

Crafts : Handmade baskets, Daniel Breillat, Rue de l'Abbaye.

Abbaye Royale St-Vincent. Wonderful animal faces decorate the façade of the 11th-century abbey church (restored 100 years ago). The Augustinian monks who lived here were involved in the draining of the marshland to the south, particularly in the digging of the "Canal des 5 Abbés" (see Chaillé-les-Marais, page 61) around 1217. The highlight of the abbey is the magnificently complete cloister of white stone opening off the chapter-house, dating from 1068, the only one in the region to remain in such a perfect state of preservation. In the summer months there are often plays, son-et-lumière performances, and concerts of Gregorian chant. ♯ 15 Mar-15 Oct, daily 10am-noon & 2.30-6pm (1 July-31 Aug, guided tours 9am-noon & 2-7pm). Tél : 51 52 49 03. 10F, children 5F.

Maison de la Meunerie. As well as learning, via sound and light presentations, how this restored watermill functioned in its heyday, you can also visit the living-quarters of the miller and his family, charmingly furnished in traditional Vendean style, and a clogmaker's workshop. During July and August local food specialities are on sale in the barn. ♯ 1 May-30 Sept ; Sat, Sun 3-7pm (1 July-31 Aug, daily 10.30am-12.30pm & 3-7pm). 16, Rue du Moulin (tel : 51 52 47 43). 18F, children 10F.

Site Néolithique Champ-Durand. Discovered from aerial views in 1971, this earth-and-stone fortification, just south of the village on the Oulmes road, dates from around 2400BC. Early men used deer-antlers and the shoulderblades of cattle to dig the two kilometres of ditches and stone walls, arranged in three concentric rings. Continuing research into the reason for its construction has shown that the site was probably also a meeting-place, a market and a graveyard. ▪

NIORT (Deux-Sèvres)

Large, flower-decorated town built of pretty, light-coloured stone on the slopes of the Sèvre Niortaise river valley, on the western borders of the area known as Green Venice (see Venise Verte, page 69). Among its picturesque, winding streets is Rue du Pont, birthplace of Madame de Maintenon, mistress and later wife of Louis XIV whom she is said to have pressured into revoking the Edict of Nantes (see Monsireigne, page 76).

The town, dominated by the twin towers of the Église St-André, is known for tanning and glove-making and, today, as an important centre of the French insurance industry. You can see 15th-century houses, and some half-timbered buildings in the network of narrow streets that includes Rue Victor-Hugo, Rue du Rabot and Rue St-Jean. At the north end of this latter stands the quaint 14th-century Pilori that was once the town hall and now houses a series of different exhibitions.

Market : Food-halls, daily ; outdoor Thursday and Saturday.

Specialities : Angelica in many forms - candied or made into jams and liqueur, "tourteau fromagé" (a sort of cheesecake made from goat's cheese), eels.

Donjon. The vast, grey, Romanesque keep looming above the river (constructed by the English kings Henry II and Richard I) contains a museum of archaeological discoveries and local history - including a typical Poitevin interior and descriptions of the glove and tanning industries. You can enjoy panoramic views of the town from the terraces. ▪ Wed-Mon 9am-noon & 2-5pm (1 May-14 Sept, Wed-Mon 9am-noon & 2-6pm). Closed on winter & spring public holidays. Quai de la Préfecture (tel : 49 2? 14 28). 14F (free on Wednesdays).

Musée des Beaux-Arts. Strong on Spanish and Dutch 17th- and 18th-century paintings, plus ivories, enamels, tapestries, and panels painted with Biblical scenes. ▪ Wed

Mon 9am-noon & 2-5pm (1 May-14 Sept, Wed-Mon 9am-noon & 2-6pm). Closed on winter & spring public holidays. Rue de l'Abreuvoir (tel : 49 24 97 84). 14F (free on Wednesdays).

Les Ruralies. A distinct improvement on British motorway service stations, this complex on the edge of the A10 autoroute, 11km east of Niort, is designed to refresh motorists by tempting them to buy regional food, and to enjoy games, picnic areas, and a large museum of agricultural life (see below).

Musée Agricole. An agricultural museum showing farm machinery, the operation of cider and oil presses, distilling equipment, harvesting and threshing machines, and a wall of bees behind glass to explain the workings of a hive. ■ Daily 10am-6pm (16 June-15 Sept, daily 10am-7pm). Les Ruralies (tel : 49 75 68 27). 20F, children 10F.

Maison des Ruralies. Films, videos and exhibitions on man and his impact on the Poitou-Charentes region. ■ Mon-Fri 10am-6pm ; Sat, Sun & public holidays 10am-7pm (1 Apr-15 Sept, daily 10am-8pm). Free.

POITIERS (Vienne)

Although this city is some 80km from the eastern edge of the Vendée, you may consider making a trip there to visit the brilliantly-conceived theme park of Futuroscope that lies 8km to the north, on the east side of the A10 autoroute. The old part of the town is almost encircled by the Clain and Boivre rivers. If you venture into the centre do not miss the intricately sculpted façade of the Romanesque church of Notre-Dame and the curious pointed roofs on its twin towers. The gothic cathedral of St-Pierre is decorated with 12th-century stained glass in vibrant reds and blues. Nearby, there are Romanesque and gothic wall-paintings in the Baptistère St-Jean.

Futuroscope. You need an entire day - maybe even more - to visit everything in the gigantic "European cinema park" at Jaunay-Clan. The history of sound and pictures is explained through state-of-the-art visual images in the Communication Pavilion. The very latest in screen entertainment includes 3D, cinema in 360° and the largest flat screen in Europe. You can experience the sensation of taking off on a space mission inside the dome-shaped Omnimax or marvel at the (sometimes terrifying) "dynamic motion theatre" where the seats move as you "drive" a racing car or "ride" a swooping rollercoaster. Elsewhere you can try a unique "magic carpet" where images are projected simultaneously in front of your eyes and several metres beneath your feet, or the Imax Solido by which you can experience virtual reality behind a pair of special electronic spectacles.

Open-air family attractions include bumper-boats, remote-controlled cars, slides, adventure playgrounds and a maze whose "walls" are made of jets of water, while indoors you can watch animated Lego models, create harmony in the "musical house" or influence the outcome of interactive cinema shows. On Saturday evenings from April to late October (and daily in July and August) visitors can also see a spectacular laser show with fountains. ♯ Mid-Feb-31 Oct, daily 9am-6pm (2 Apr-1 July, daily 9am-7pm ; 2-31 July, daily 9am-8pm ; 1 Aug-3 Sept, daily 9am-9pm). Laser shows early Apr-end Oct, Sat (July and Aug, daily) 10pm. Tel : 49 49 30 80 ; fax reservations 49 49 30 25. 135F, children 100F ; two-day ticket 230F, children 170F.

LA POMMERAIE-SUR-SEVRE

Attractive village on the eastern boundary of the Vendée, 9km north-east of Pouzauges, where two picturesque old bridges cross the Sèvre Nantaise river.

Church. Beneath the elegant, Plantagenet-style vaulting, is the church's treasure - the Renaissance frescoes along the south wall that depict, in witty style, the Seven Deadly Sins as a procession of animals and colourfully-clad people. A mini sound-and-light show in French explains the sequence. ▪

POUZAUGES

You need to be extremely adept at hill-starts to drive around the narrow streets in the centre of this attractive town nicknamed "the pearl of the bocage". A ruined, 13th-century castle that belonged to the notorious Gilles de Rais (see Tiffauges, page 94) occupies the highest point, with a granite cross commemorating 32 hostages who were executed in the courtyard during the Vendée wars.

Market : Thursday.

Specialities : Fleury-Michon pork products, obtainable in supermarkets everywhere - even Britain.

Église Notre-Dame du Vieux-Pouzauges. Well signposted, about 1km south-east of the town, the church of Notre-Dame (completed in around 1066) stands in a grassy churchyard. Once inside, press a button for a seven-minute son-et-lumière performance highlighting the magnificent wall-paintings on the north side of the nave. A symphony of terracotta and ochre, they are thought to date from the 13th century but they were not rediscovered under layers of paint until 1948. The French commentary explains the subjects. Five scenes on the lower level depict episodes in the the life of the Virgin Mary and her parents : an angel appearing to her father ; the kiss between him and his wife at the Golden Gate of Jerusalem ; two pictures of Mary in the Temple, and one of an angel appearing to her. Above are friezes of grotesque animals and illustrations representing different months of the year. Over the west door are more-recently uncovered frescoes showing Cain and Abel. ▪

Moulins du Terrier-Marteau. On an exposed ridge 1km north of the town, just off the road to Les Herbiers, stand two handsome windmills. Restored to activity in the 1980s, they have been re-equipped with canvas-covered sails that turn gracefully as traditionally-dressed millers give visitors a tour, explaining the process from hoisting the sacks of corn to the top to bagging the finished flour at the bottom. Around the top of the hill are some picturesque walks and panoramic views. ♯ Mid-May-mid-Sept ; Sat, Sun 3-7pm (1 July-31 Aug, Thurs-Sun & public holidays, 3-7pm). Tel : 51 57 52 83. 12F

Bois de la Folie. Mysterious hilltop clump of trees, reputed to be inhabited by the fairy Mélusine (see Vouvant, page 82) and numerous pixies and goblins, just beyond the Terrier-Marteau windmills, where Druids are said to have worshipped the mistletoe. On a clear day you may be able to glimpse the sea, 75km to the west. ▪

Puy Crapaud. At 269 metres, this hill just to the south-east of Pouzauges is one of the highest points in the Vendée. From the top of an old windmill at the summit you have a superb view along the range of Vendean hills stretching north and south. ▪

RÉAUMUR

Pretty village 8km south of Pouzauges, with an interesting fortified gothic church and pleasant walks along the river Lay.

Manoir de Réaumur. A 17th-century manor house containing a permanent exhibition on the life of René-Antoine Ferchault de Réaumur (1683-1757), the versatile French scientist who devised a reliable way of measuring temperature. He was bor in La Rochelle, but spent holidays at this country mansion which belonged to his family. As well as inventing the thermometer that bears his name (on which freezing-point is 0˚ and boiling-point 80˚), Réaumur also developed a method of tinning iron, and his studies of insect life made him the father of French entomology. ⊞ 1 May-1 Nov, Sun & public holidays 2.30-6pm (last Mon of June to last Sun of Aug, daily 2.30-7pm). Tel : 51 57 90 99. 20F, children free.

ST-MESMIN

Small village near the eastern boundary of the Vendée, 5km east of Pouzauges.

Château de St-Mesmin-la-Ville. About 1km north-east of the main village, and just across the departmental boundary, is this impressive, partly-ruined, 14th-century castle, overlooking a tributary of the Sèvre Nantaise river. From its inner courtyard you can visit the chapel and some of the rooms in the tower above, and enjoy the view from the rampart that runs around the top. DIY plumbers will be interested in the sewage-disposal system - state-of-the-art for its time - that leads directly into the moat. ⊞ 1 May-11 Nov, Sun & public holidays 2.30-6pm (last Mon of June to last Sun of Aug, daily 2.30-7pm). Tel : 51 66 40 96. 20F, children free.

ST-MICHEL-LE-CLOUCQ

Village 6km north-east of Fontenay-le-Comte.

Brocante : Emmaüs - part of a highly successful network of enormous junk shops set up by a French priest, Abbé Pierre, to sell donated goods and to be run by and on behalf of down-and-outs. ■ Mon 2-6pm, Tues-Sat 8am-noon & 2-6pm.

Parc Ornithologique de Pagnole. Cassowaries, cranes, macaws, ostriches and other exotic birds can be seen alongside llamas and more ordinary species, like donkeys, in this flower-filled park, 3km north of the village. ⊞ 1 Apr-30 Nov, daily 9am-dusk. La Braud (tel : 51 69 02 55). 28F, children 14F.

Lac d'Albert. You can swim, windsurf and rent pedaloes in the summer months at this large lake on the river Vendée, 4km west of the village towards Chassenon-le-Bourg. During the holidays there are also children's games and a bar. ■

ST-MICHEL-MONT-MERCURE

Picturesque village - the highest in the Vendée - 14km north-west of Pouzauges. The late-19th-century church (which you can climb for a wonderful panoramic view on a clear day) is crowned with a massive copper statue of St Michael.

Market : Monday.

Moulin des Justices. Imposing 19th-century windmill, 3km north-west of St-Michel. Still in working order, its adjustable, slatted sails creak round producing wholemeal flour as the miller explains the finer points of operation in a half-hour guided tour. You can buy bread, flour and biscuits to take away, or try sweet and savoury pancakes in the crêperie next door. ■ Sat, Sun & bank holidays 3-5pm (15 June-15 Sept, daily 3-7pm). Tel : 51 57 80 84. 15F, children 10F.

ST-PROUANT

Village, 10km south-west of Pouzauges. Footpaths lead through the forest of La Plissonnière to the north, where mushroom-hunters search for ceps and other delectable fungi in the autumn.

Prieuré de Chassay-Grammont. Standing proudly above the surrounding country-side, 7km south-west of St-Prouant, is the magnificently preserved 12th-century monastery founded by Richard the Lionheart in 1196 as a place of worship for some 10 monks of the Grandmont order. In spite of having been used as a farm in the late 17th century, before being sold off after the Revolution, the tall chapel and abbey buildings are in remarkably good condition, forming a complete, harmonious group around the cloister. The chapter-house and refectory both have elegantly vaulted ceilings in Plantagenet style. The abbey contains an exhibition on the history of the hermit-like Grandmont monks who took vows of poverty, humility and chastity. Occasional concerts of classical music are held during the summer. ♯ 1 May-11 Nov, Sun & public holidays 2-6pm (20 June-31 Aug, daily 2.30-7pm). Tel : 51 66 40 96. 20F, students 15F, children free.

SIGOURNAIS

Picturesque village 8km north-east of Chantonnay. High stone walls surround an enormous, beautifully restored medieval castle keep, with pointed, slate-roofed turrets, and a covered gallery with narrow slits for the defenders' arrows. Apart from the "Journées du Patrimoine" (National Heritage Days) in mid-September each year - when you can have a guided tour of the interior - it is not open to visitors, but remains an impressive sight, even from the outside.

As a sad comparison, and an indication of the enormous cost and effort involved in restoring old buildings, take a look at the village's other castle - a building of similar age overlooking the water-meadows on the western side of the village. Almost invisible under a blanket of ivy, the walls and the slate-less woodwork of its turrets are collapsing into oblivion.

VOUVANT

A small place, 12km north of Fontenay-le-Comte, so pretty that it could be a film set. Overhead cables have been banished, along with some of the other signs of the 20th century, the roads have been newly cobbled - all in all, it certainly deserves its accolade as one of France's most beautiful villages. High on a promontory in a crook of the river Mère, Vouvant is surrounded by medieval walls from which you can look down on the meandering waterway below. Crowds throng here in the summer to admire the famous façade of the church (see below), drink in the medieval atmosphere and to buy interesting crafts. At the crêperie on the opposite bank you can rent pedaloes to use on the river.

Festivals : Fête folklorique (festival of folk-dancing and traditions), early August.

Romanesque church. The richly-sculpted decoration on the north front is one of th marvels of the Vendée. Fantastical animals surround the doorways. Above is a serie of magnificent statues dating from the 15th century. Inside, the ornamentation is sim pler ; you can have a closer look at some stone carvings in the 11th-century crypt. ■

Tour Mélusine. Ancient watch-tower that dominates the village and surroundir countryside built, according to folklore, in 1242 by the fairy Mélusine.

This legendary creature, who had been sentenced by a curse to become half-serpe each Saturday, has been credited with the construction of several mighty castles, eac within the space of a single night. Some say her name is a corruption of "Mèr Lusignan", and that she married into a powerful local family of that name in ancier times. Before agreeing to marriage, however, she made it a condition that her husban should never see her on Saturdays. He agreed but one day, mad with jealousy, he spie on her. On glimpsing his naked wife bathing, he saw to his amazement, that she had a serpent's tail. Realising her secret was out, Mélusine flew through the window, never to be seen again, and all her works crumbled...

However, enough of the stone steps remain to allow you to enjoy a spectacular view from the top. ∎

CHAPTER 5

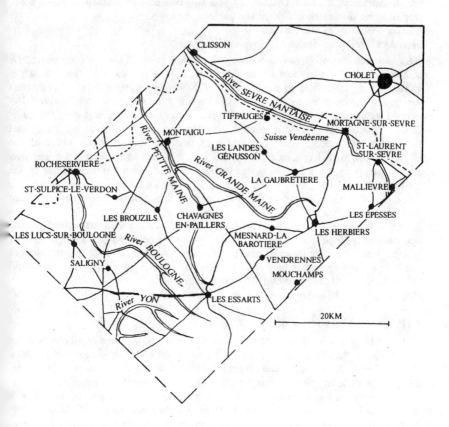

⌐ES BROUZILS

⌐mall village, 12km south of Montaigu.

⌐estival : Foire à la Mogette (haricot bean festival), mid-October.

⌐efuge de Grasla. Signposts point the way to a site deep in the forest, 2km south-east ⌐f the village, where in 1794 almost 2,500 survivors from local families took shelter ⌐fter the colonnes infernales (see page 27) had destroyed their homes during the Wars ⌐f the Vendée. Local volunteers have reconstructed rustic shelters of wood and ⌐eather as well as a chapel and workshops to show such crafts as charcoal-burning ⌐nd blacksmithing. Maps and a 20-minute video help to put you in the picture.

Nearby is a memorial cross to General Charette, the Vendean leader, who often concealed his troops in this impenetrable woodland. Guided tours available. Forest walks and shady picnic spots. ♯ 1 Apr-end Nov, Tues-Sat 3-6pm, Sun 3-7pm. Tel : 51 42 35 29. 10F.

CHAVAGNES-EN-PAILLERS

A profusion of bell-towers and churches indicates that this small town 12km south-east of Montaigu is one of the Vendée's "holy places". In 1801 the parish priest, Father Baudouin, founded a seminary and two convents in Chavagnes - the solid, imposing buildings that still dominate parts of the town.
Market : Wednesday and Saturday.
Festival : Foire à la Brioche, third weekend in May.

Sanctuaire de Notre-Dame-de-Salette. About 5km south of the town, by way of La Rabatelière, stands the most extraordinary sight. Just off the D17 that leaves the village of La Rabatelière in the direction of St-Fulgent teeter at least 20 enormous towers and turrets of stone and brick, built in 1889 and interspersed with colourfully-painted statues representing visions that appeared to two children in eastern France in 1846. The whole thing is built on an impossibly steep slope, but is so intriguing that anybody nimble enough should scramble up past the Stations of the Cross to the simple chapel, built like a castle keep. Inside is a tall, plain wooden cross, and two statues, plus a photograph of a swarm of bees that settled on the head of one of the outdoor figures in the 1980s. If you really have a head for heights, you can climb up a taller, slightly rickety tower to the side (open on Sundays and bank holidays from 3-6pm).
It's safer to descend the hillside by the series of steps, which also gives you an opportunity to look more closely at the charming, coloured statues arranged in groups. Just across the road at the bottom is a pretty, tree-lined stream. Notices remind you to respect this holy place so, however tempting the idea, children should not make unseemly noise or climb on the monuments. ■
Pilgrimage : First Sunday in September.

CHOLET (Maine-et-Loire)

Although lying just to the east of the Vendée's boundary, the town of Cholet declares itself to be the "capitale historique de la Vendée militaire" (historic capital of military Vendée), for the ferocious Vendean wars involved much of the département of Maine-et-Loire as well. In spite of being sacked and burnt three times during the post-Revolution years, the town centre retains a number of picturesque mansions with ironwork balconies, once the homes of wealthy cloth merchants. Until 1793 "toiles" (textiles) made the city's fortune ; today the emphasis is on the manufacture of ready-to-wear garments and the making of shoes. The main shopping streets are clustered around the twin-spired, 19th-century church of Notre-Dame.
The strange claim to be also the "capitale du mouchoir" (capital of the handkerchief) comes from the heyday of the town's textile industry when this was one of the specialities manufactured here. However, this humble, everday item shot to prominence in 1900 when Théodore Botrel, a celebrated Breton cabaret artist, created stirring romantic song called "Le Mouchoir rouge de Cholet" (The Red Handkerchief of Cholet). In it he sang of a soldier who has bought three white Cholet handkerchiefs as a present for his true love. Before he can give them to her General Charette, the Vendean war hero, requisitions them, using one to wear on his head, one to hold his

sword, and pinning the third over his heart to become red with his blood. Such was the success of the song, that the town's enterprising firm began to turn out handkerchiefs of blood-red, bordered with white (the identifying colour worn by the Vendeans). These became an established feature, and can today be bought from La Bonne Toile de Cholet at 2 Avenue Gambetta.

Market : Saturday, 8am-5pm.

Festival : Carnival, early April (illuminated procession on the following Saturday).

Musée d'art et d'histoire. Opened only in February 1993, this ultra-modern museum is devoted largely to the Vendée wars and the city's role in them (more than 50 per cent of its population was killed in the four years of fighting). Exhibits include weapons, objects and dramatic 19th-century paintings. Other displays feature 18th- and 19th-century sculpture, and a number of contemporary geometrical works. ▪ Wed-Mon 10am-noon & 2-5pm. 2 Avenue de l'Abreuvoir (tel : 41 49 29 00). Free.

Parc de Loisirs de Ribou. Large lake 3km south-east of the town, with walking, fishing, tennis and watersports during the summer. Nearby is an ornithological reserve on Lac du Verdon. ▪

Musée Paysan. Located on the D20, south-east of Cholet on the Poitiers road, the museum shows a typical interior of a late-19th-century farmhouse in the Mauges region, with furniture and contemporary tools. ▪ Wed-Mon 3-6pm. Closed on public holidays. La Goubaudière, Port de Ribou (tel : 41 58 00 83). Free.

Parc Oriental. Created in 1900 by a Paris architect who adored the Far East, this park, 13km south-east of Cholet, is inspired by the Japanese parks of the 17th century. Its 120 species include magnolias, maples and pines in what is claimed to be the largest Japanese-style garden in Europe. ▪ Tues-Sun 2-6pm (1 July-31 Aug, daily 9am-noon & 2-6pm). Château Colbert Hotel, Maulévrier (tel : 41 55 50 14). 13F.

CLISSON (Loire-Atlantique)

Your first impression on glimpsing this attractive town on the banks of the Sèvre Nantaise river, some 25km west of Cholet and on the northernmost border of the Vendée, is of having somehow strayed into a corner of Italy - an unexpected side-effect of the Vendée wars. The Republicans' ruthlessly efficient fire-and-sword policy ruined the castle and flattened the town in 1794, leaving just two ancient bridges across the Sèvre and its tributary the Moine. The rebuilding was started in Italianate style by the wealthy Cacault brothers - Pierre and François - and Frédéric Lemot, a sculptor whom they had known in Italy. The idea caught local imagination and from the early 19th century a harmonious collection of buildings grew up on the slopes above the two rivers - even the owners of some of the factories along the banks built in the same delicate Italian style. Floodlit on summer nights, Clisson takes on an even more magical quality.

Waymarked footpaths lead along the banks of the Sèvre from Le Pallet in the north to Tiffauges in the south. The tourist office arranges guided tours of the town and some of its local industries. Since this is serious Muscadet country, the bureau also offers a "Guide des Étapes en Muscadet" to tell you where to find the wine producers and the "dégustations" (wine-tastings).

Signposted drives include the "Route historique des Marches de Bretagne" (historic route along the Breton Marches or borders) indicating the fortresses strung out, from Clisson as far as Mont-St-Michel on the Channel coast, to protect the frontier between the powerful duchy of Brittany and the kingdom of France until the two were united by the marriage of King Charles VIII with Anne of Brittany in 1491. The

"Route Touristique du Vignoble du Val de Loire" (a trail through the wine-producing areas of the Loire Valley) takes you through the vineyards producing Muscadet, Gros-Plant du Pays Nantais and Coteaux d'Ancenis between Clisson and the town of Saumur, 100km to the east, on the river Loire.

Market : Friday.

Festival : Baroque music in the town's churches and in the Villa Lemot (see below) in July and August.

Specialities : Muscadet de Sèvre-et-Maine and Gros-Plant wines.

Château de Clisson. The successive enclosures and improvements that were carried out between the 12th and 16th centuries make this stronghold - now a dramatic ruin overlooking the town - an excellent example of military architecture. In one of the courtyards, 18 of the town's inhabitants perished when they were thrown into a well by Republicans in 1794. There is a son-et-lumière show in August. ▪ Wed-Mon 9.30am-noon & 2-6pm (1 Mar-30 Nov, daily 9.30am-noon & 2-6pm). Tel : 40 54 02 22. 13F, children 10F.

Les Halles. The town's market hall lies between the castle and the nearby church. Wander inside, and look up at the incredible network of 15th-century wooden beams that make up its roof. The building is said to have survived the town's destruction only because of its usefulness as a temporary barracks during the Vendean wars. ▪

Garenne Lemot. Large park studded with follies, statues, temples and grottoes on the east bank of the Sèvre, designed by the sculptor Frédéric Lemot (1771-1827) as his own country retreat. ▪ Daily 9am-6pm (1 Apr-30 Sept, daily 9am-8pm). Free.

Maison du Jardinier. Charming, Italian-style, rustic building at the park entrance containing an exhibition showing the Italian influences on the town's architecture. ▪ Tues-Sun 10am-1pm & 2-6pm (1 Apr-30 Sept, daily 10am-1pm & 2-6pm). Tel : 40 03 96 79.

Villa Lemot. An elegant building open for temporary art exhibitions. From the villa's terrace you can glimpse on the other side of the river the Temple de l'Amitié, burial place of the sculptor whose vision is so indelibly stamped on the town. ▪ Daily, during exhibitions, 10am-1pm & 2-6pm. Tel : 40 03 92 60.

Base de Moulin-Plessard. In summer you can hire mountain-bikes at this water sports area on the river, opposite the Garenne Lemot (see above). ⧓

LES ÉPESSES

This small village in the haut-bocage, 10km north-east of Les Herbiers, is the focus for some of the département's best-known entertainment at the world-famous castle of Le Puy-du-Fou (see below).

Train à vapeur. Steam swirls once more around the station building 5km to the south west of the village now that enthusiasts have reopened a 22km section of line between Les Herbiers, Les Épesses and Mortagne-sur-Sèvre. You can now board steam train at either of the stations and enjoy a one-hour journey alongside green fields, across dramatic viaducts and through the Vendean hills (two return trips a made per day). On certain occasions you can even book a meal to be served in a Orient-Express carriage. ⧓ 1 June-15 Sept, Wed, Fri, Sat, Sun & public holiday 3.15-5.15pm ; 16-30 Sept, Sun 3.15-5.15pm. Tel : 51 57 64 64. Single 45F, children 30F return 60F & 40F

Musée de l'Histoire du Chemin de Fer en Vendée. The station at Les Épesses (see above) is now the Vendée railway museum, displaying photographs, posters an documents recalling bygone times. ⌗ 1 June-15 Sept, Wed, Fri, Sat, Sun & public holidays 3.15-5.15pm ; 16-30 Sept, Sun 3.15-5.15pm. Tel : 51 92 92 92. 5F

Puy-du-Fou. Lying 2km north-west of Les Épesses is the ruined granite-and-brick Renaissance castle, burnt down by Republicans in 1794, whose name has become synonymous with the dazzling "Cinéscénie" (see below), the sound and light show staged there in the summer months. In addition, there is a museum and a theme park (see below), so plenty to entertain the whole family for an entire day before the performance starts.

Écomusée de la Vendée. In the most complete remaining wing of the 15th- to 16th-century castle of Puy-du-Fou is a museum of Vendean history from prehistoric times up to the present day, and that of the castle itself. There are fine examples of Romanesque stone-carving, and explanations of the Wars of Religion that pitched Catholics against Protestants throughout the Renaissance period in the Bas-Poitou (as the Vendée was known until the time of the Revolution). An ingeniously illuminated model of the Vendée, Brittany and Maine-et-Loire illustrates, with sound effects, the start of the Vendean uprising that evolved into the Vendée wars (you will get more from this if you first read the section on page 24). ⌗ 1 Feb-31 Dec, Tues-Sun 10am-noon, 2-6pm (1 May-30 Sept, Tues-Sun 10am-7pm). Tel : 51 64 11 11. 12F

Grand Parcours. You can spend a whole day savouring the atmosphere of a recon-structed 18th-century Vendean village at Puy-du-Fou that includes an example of the type of sunken country lane where the Blancs (Vendeans) liked to stage bloody ambushes on the Republican troops. A busy programme of events is on offer with costumed entertainers juggling and jousting, and demonstrations of falconry, stunt-riding, baking, spinning and rural crafts. The only drawback is that you are not allowed to picnic in the 30 hectares of woods and fields (though you may leave to eat your sandwiches in the car park, and be re-admitted later). ⌗ 1-31 May, Sun & bank holidays 10am-7pm ; 1 June-12 Sept, Tues-Sun 10am-7pm. Tel : 51 64 11 11. 75F, children 35F

Cinéscénie : "Jacques Maupillier, paysan vendéen". Some 200,000 spectators a year come to see this incredible open-air, night-time show, first performed in 1977. More than 700 people and 50 horsemen from neighbouring communes act out the story of the Vendée through the life of "Jacques Maupillier", a Vendean peasant, to the accompaniment of lasers, fountains, fireworks and the most sophisticated sound and lighting techniques. Although the commentary (using the voices of famous French actors like Philippe Noiret) is entirely in French - unless you manage to book one of 50 specially-equipped seats that offer versions in other languages - the overall visual effect is so breathtaking that total understanding of the story hardly matters. Galloping horses thunder out of the castle to fall over at your feet, ballet dancers perform seemingly upon the very surface of the lake, sudden bursts of light reveal hundreds of actors who have composed themselves into living tableaux in the darkness. The picturesque castle and its lake provide the backdrop to this thrilling spectacle, the ultimate in son-et-lumière performances.

You need to book early since there are only about 20 performances a year, but note that the show continues whatever the weather and absolutely no refunds are made. Seating is on wooden grandstands which are no barrier to the breezes that can whistle across the lake even on the warmest night, so dress warmly and take rugs or sleeping-bags to cover legs - large plastic bin-liners are a wise choice to keep each member of the family dry if it looks like rain. Arrive at least one hour before the start to find your seats. Rather than drive yourself a long distance late at night you can book a complete package, sometimes at a few days' notice, that includes coach transport from far-flung towns and villages on the coast and elsewhere - enquire at local tourist offices. It's no good relying on buying a seat at the gate on the day. ⧧ June-Sept, mostly Fri & Sat. June/July starts 10.30pm, Aug/Sept starts 10pm ; the show runs about 1hr 40 mins. Tel : 51 64 11 11. 110F, children 35F.

LES ESSARTS

Industrial and market town 20km south-west of Les Herbiers.
Market : Wednesday and Saturday.
Château des Essarts. Feudal castle visited by the future Henri IV when he was Henri of Navarre in 1588, of which the 11th-century tower is all that remains. An attractive park surrounds the ruins. ⧧ 15 June-15 Sept, daily 10am-noon & 2-6pm. Tel : 51 62 88 86. 10F, children free.
Parish church. Beneath the 19th-century church is the Romanesque crypt of an ancient priory, an underground passageway decorated with frescoes and lined with sculpted pillars. ■

LA GAUBRETIERE

Known as the "Pantheon of the Vendée", this village 9km north-west of Les Herbiers is the resting-place of many who served in the Vendean uprising. During the war and its reprisals the village lost 1,200 of its 1,700 population. These victims and some of the Vendée leaders are buried in the cemetery, either in large family tombs or beneath a granite obelisk in a mass grave (a plan of the plots is available from the Mairie nearby). In the centre of the village is a memorial to General Charles-Henri Sapinaud, one of the Vendean generals, who miraculously survived the war and died in 1829 after having been the village's first mayor. ■
Château de Landebaudière. Somewhat austere 18th-century mansion a short distance to the north-west of the village, surrounded by a park of peaceful, tree-lined avenues. The Duc d'Elbée was married here in 1788 ; the château also sheltered the Marquis de Bonchamps after he had been wounded in battle. The house is open only for a temporary exhibition in 1994. * 1 June-1 Sept, Tues-Sun 2-6pm. Tel : 51 67 10 21. Free

LES HERBIERS

Town at the north-west end of the Collines Vendéennes (Vendean Hills), overlooking the Grand Maine river 25km south-west of Cholet. Among its many industries is the world-renowned boatbuilding company of Jeanneau, which in 1994 supplied Kevin Costner with two trimarans for a futuristic new feature film.
Market : Thursday and Saturday.
Train à vapeur. The town is the southern terminus for the steam train that runs via Les Épesses to Mortagne-sur-Sèvre (see Les Épesses, page 86). ⧧ 1 June-15 Sept, Wed, Fri, Sat, Sun & public holidays 3.15-5.15pm ; 16-30 Sept, Sun 3.15-5.15pm. Tel : 51 5 64 64. Single 45F, children 30F ; return 60F & 40F.
Mont des Alouettes. A high point (231m) on the Cholet road, 3km north of Les Herbiers, this windy ridge is considered the gateway to the Vendée. When you stand in the shadow of the three tall windmills (all that remain of the seven which once stood here) and gaze at the vast panorama of greenery on all sides you can appreciate how useful a semaphore point it was to the Vendean forces. Hidden in the undulating wooded bocage, they could tell the enemy's movements from a code that depended

on the position in which the mills' sails were parked - signs included X for "all clear" and + for "alert". A 19th-century chapel commemorates the wars. ■

Château d'Ardelay. A striking, square tower with a distinctive, red-tiled, pointed roof dominates the village of Ardelay, 3km south of Les Herbiers. It makes up one corner of a walled courtyard that includes a handsome "logis seigneurial" or lord's house, now used for occasional exhibitions. You can clatter over the wooden drawbridge that spans the dry moat and visit the elegantly-restored rooms of the tower - empty but for some magnificent granite fireplaces. The wonderful array of timbers that support the steeply-pitched roof are visible on the top floor. ■ Sat, Sun (during exhibitions) 2.30-6.30pm (1 June-30 Sept, Wed-Mon 3-7pm). Tel : 51 66 95 41. 10F, children 5F.

Abbaye de Notre-Dame de la Grainetière. Founded in 1130 by Benedictine monks, the abbey 8km south-west of Les Herbiers was fortified, and withstood an English seige in 1372. (Students of French literature may like to know that Abbé Prévost wrote several chapters of his sentimental novel "Manon Lescaut" here, around 1731.) The abbey's fortunes declined and the building was severely damaged by the Protestants during the Wars of Religion, being reduced to further ruin in the aftermath of the Revolution and the Vendée wars when it was sold off for use as a quarry and farm. One side of its stone-flagged gothic cloister remains, supported on a series of graceful twin columns ; the only other surviving feature is a magnificent vaulted "salle capitulaire" (chapter-house). Since the late 1970s, a small group of Benedictine monks has returned. They offer guided tours by appointment, though you can wander around and admire the building by yourself. ■ Tues-Sun 9am-noon & 2.30-7pm. Tel : 51 67 21 19. 10F, children 2F.

LES LANDES-GÉNUSSON
Village 14km north-west of Les Herbiers.

Les Boucheries. A little west of the village, three lakes spread over a total area of 30 hectares make up this wetland which is home to quantities of grebe, duck, moorhens, herons and geese and an important staging-post for many more exotic migrating waterfowl. The Maison de l'Étang gives information about the resident and visiting birds and the opportunity to have a closer look at them through a telescope from a nearby observatory. In July and August you can fish (with appropriate permit, see page 12). ■ Daily 8am-noon & 1.30pm-dusk. Tel : 51 91 72 25. Free.

LES LUCS-SUR-BOULOGNE
On 23 February 1794 the Republican colonnes infernales (see page 27) wiped out 564 women, children and old people as they knelt in a hilltop chapel where they had sought sanctuary. Today the village, 23km north of La Roche-sur-Yon, contains a shrine not only to their memory but to that of all who fell in the long, post-Revolution civil war.

Chemin de la Mémoire. Opened for the 1993 bicentenary of the wars, this low, grey, slab-sided hall of memory 1km north-east of the village centre at the foot of the hill crowned by the Petit-Luc chapel, has aroused considerable local controversy, yet the mistake is to think of it as a museum.

Small, knee-high panels identifying some of the wars' leading figures line the path to a wooden footbridge that spans a moat surrounding this state-of-the-art memorial building. Inside, using a strictly minimalist approach, the designers have spotlit just a few, exquisitely-chosen items - though you need a torch to read the tiny labels that lurk in the dark beside them and certainly would find it helpful to know something about the characters and events beforehand (see page 24). However, once you let the hypnotic music seep inside you, the overall effect is extremely moving. Roughly-crayoned abstract sketches are projected in succession to suggest the murders, fire and pillage of this march of terror. Leaving the slide presentation, you are immediately confronted by real examples of the menacing weapons that the peasants improvised from their scythes and hedging tools, turning around the blades to convert them into lethal bayonets.

As you emerge, blinking and somewhat subdued, into the daylight, you climb the wooded slope to the chapel of Petit-Luc (built in 1867 on the site of the massacre from the stones of the original) that contains marble panels bearing the name of every one of 563 dead - the 564th, Abbé Voyneau the village priest, is comme-morated farther on by a simple stone column. ▪ Wed-Mon 10am-6pm (1 Apr-31 Oct, daily 10am-6pm ; 1 May-31 Aug, daily 10am-7pm). Tel : 51 42 81 00. Free.

Église St-Pierre. The stained-glass windows in the village church tell the tale of the tragic events that took place in the chapel on the hill (see above). ▪

MALLIEVRE

The remains of a feudal castle overlook this attractive, granite-built village on the Sèvre Nantaise river 15km north-east of Les Herbiers. Its narrow, sloping streets are bordered by houses once inhabited by weavers and weaving-masters. One steep street leads to a weaver's cellar where you can sometimes see one of the remaining craftsmen at work. Nearby are signposted routes around the hills and dales of the "Suisse Vendéenne" (see page 94), and the valley of the Sèvre Nantaise.

Maison de l'Eau. Films, models and aquariums lead you through the story of water -- so essential to life - in the house of a former weaving-master. They provide explana-tions of how man has used this element to power industry, to make paper and flour, to create defensive moats and spectacular fountains, and to develop leisure activities. You can also sniff different "eaux" - "eau de javel" (bleach), "eau écarlate" (grease-spot remover) and so on. ⊭ 1 May-30 Sept, Mon-Fri 2-7pm ; Sat, Sun 2-8pm. 7 Rue de la Poterne (tel : 51 65 33 99). 30F.

MESNARD-LA-BAROTIERE

Village 8km west of Les Herbiers.

Vieille église St-Christophe. On the edge of the village is a charming 11th-century church that contains some wonderful medieval wall-paintings, discovered in 1950 and restored 40 years later. Even the most bloodthirsty of children may flinch at the 13th century depictions of a saint being barbecued over blazing logs, or the beheading of John the Baptist. Less gruesome panels include the Annunciation, the Nativity and the Last Supper and, an unusual feature, a scene that is presumed to show the paintings' wealthy sponsors. Tops of columns around the chancel are decorated with primitive stone carvings of leaves and roughly-hewn beasts. To see the frescoes at their best you must go in broad daylight since there is no electric lighting in the church. Some descriptive notes lie on the altar. ▪

Lac de la Tricherie. This open expanse of water 1km south of Mesnard is a popular place for swimming and fishing. Well-kept surroundings offer extra summer-time pleasures of mini-golf, crêperie, and picnic tables under shady beech and oak trees. ▪

MONTAIGU

Attractive medieval town, still partly surrounded by solid ramparts above the river Maine, 52km south-west of Cholet. Little remains of the 12th- to 15th-century castle that became strategically important under Louis XI, but there are pleasant strolls in the Jardin des Remparts or the Parc des Rochettes. Narrow streets off the main shopping thoroughfare (Rue Clemenceau) wind between ancient walls that shelter some picturesque old houses. Montaigu's tourist office, near the castle, is extremely well supplied with information both on the Vendée and nearby areas of Loire-Atlantique and the Muscadet region. At St-Georges-de-Montaigu, a couple of kilometres south-east of the town, are some delightful walks in the valley of the Grande Maine.

Market : Saturday.

Musée de Nord-Vendée. A collection of objects and documents illustrating the history of the northern part of the département, housed in a pretty 17th-century stone pavilion on the site of the medieval castle. ⌗ 1 June-30 Sept, Tues-Sat 9am-noon & 2-6pm. Pavillon des Nourrices (tel : 51 94 02 71). Free.

MORTAGNE-SUR-SEVRE

Delightful town on the Sèvre Nantaise river, at the eastern boundary of the Vendée, 15km north-east of Les Herbiers. It is dominated by the ruins of a fortress - said to have been built by the brother of William the Conqueror - partially destroyed on the orders of Cardinal Richelieu in 1626. Around the church are some interesting old streets.

Market : Tuesday.

Train à vapeur. You can take a one-hour ride on a steam train through magnificent scenery to Les Épesses (see page 86). Meals, to be served in an Orient-Express carriage - organised by the highly-reputed Hôtel de France at Mortagne - can be booked on certain trips (the train stops on a viaduct so you can enjoy the view while you are eating). ⌗ 1 June-15 Sept, Wed, Fri, Sat, Sun & public holidays 3.15-5.15pm ; 16-30 Sept, Sun 3.15-5.15pm. Tel : 51 57 64 64. Single 45F, children 30F ; return 60F & 40F.

MOUCHAMPS

Picturesque small town clinging to a hillside above the river Lay, 13km south of Les Herbiers. It is best explored on foot, as you can easily get a car stuck fast in the narrow, winding streets.

Le Colombier. The body of the French politician Georges Clemenceau was buried in 1929 next to that of his father in the grounds of this 16th-century manor house, signposted off the D13 to the east of the village. A mellow building, adorned with turrets that sprout from the corners, it had been in the hands of his family since 1749. As a ferocious left-wing politician Clemenceau was dubbed "le Tigre" (the Tiger) ; his successful negotiation of the Treaty of Versailles that brought to an end the First World War showed his undoubted statesmanship and earned him the affectionate nickname of "Père la Victoire" (Father of Victory). He was born at Mouilleron-en-Pareds (see page 76), 20 km to the south-east, and spent much of his retirement in his Vendean seaside home at St-Vincent-sur-Jard (see page 49), 22km south-east of Les Sables-d'Olonne. Beyond a gate, in the grounds, you can see the tomb of the distinguished statesman, overlooking the Petit-Lay river. ∎

ROCHESERVIERE

An attractive village in the valley of the Boulogne river 15km west of Montaigu, easily missed since the D937 sweeps past it over an enormous viaduct. The ancient packhorse bridge across the river was the site of a fierce battle between royalists and Republicans in 1793, and another round of bitter fighting in June 1815. The square around the Mairie has been recently spruced up, giving due prominence to a few 16th- and 17th-century houses, and a plaque commemorates a more peaceful event - the passage through Rocheservière in December 1991 of the Olympic flame, on its way to the winter games at Albertville. Overlooking it all is the fairy-tale Renaissance-style Château de la Touche, a riot of slate-covered pinnacles and towers. There are pleasant walks along the banks of the Boulogne to the north.

Market : Second Wednesday of the month.

Specialities : Gros-Plant, Muscadet & Gamay wines.

Church. Built in the 19th century, it has richly-coloured stained-glass windows, 10 of which illustrate episodes from the Wars of the Vendée. ■

Pierre-aux-Lutins. Just off the D7 south-east of the town is a picnic spot beside the Boulogne river. You can see a cave with an altar inside and, nearby, a large piece of rock known as the Elfin Stone. ■

Château de Bois-Chevalier. Signposted off the Legé road, 5km south-west of Rocheservière in the neighbouring département of Loire-Atlantique, stands a rarity, a stately home built in 1655 that has emerged miraculously unscathed from the troubles of the late 18th century. During the Wars of the Vendée it belonged to royalist sympathisers ; General Charette, whose headquarters were for a time at nearby Legé, was a frequent visitor and used to hold parties in the drawing-room. Its higgledy-piggledy slate roofs are reflected in the still waters of the moat that surrounds the house. Inside, a 45-minute guided tour (with accompanying notes in delightfully fractured English) takes you from dining-room to attics of what is still essentially a family home. ♯ 1 Apr-30 Sept, daily 9.30am-noon & 2-7pm. Tel : 40 26 62 18. 18F

ST-LAURENT-SUR-SEVRE

The "holy town" of the Vendée lies 11km south of Cholet in a curve of the Sèvre Nantaise river, on the eastern edge of the département. Since the death here in 1716 of St Louis-Marie Grignion de Montfort (see Mervent, page 75), a Breton missionary priest, St-Laurent has become a place of pilgrimage and a centre for the religious groups that he founded.

The saint's tomb is in the 19th-century basilica. Among other notable buildings are the Maison du St-Esprit, home to an order of Montfortian missionaries, and, opposite, the Maison Mère des Filles de la Sagesse - the headquarters of an order of nuns who care for the sick.

Parc de la Barbinière. Large park on the wooded slopes above the meandering river, just to the west of the town. Little islands dot the water, and by the bank is a restored watermill (however, although the wheel turns picturesquely, there is nothing worthy of visit inside). On summer afternoons you can see the Les Épesses-to-Mortagne steam train (see pages 86 and 91) puff over the viaduct. ■

ST-SULPICE-LE-VERDON

Lying 13.5km south-west of Montaigu, this large village is an important point on the Vendée Memorial map because of the nearby country house of La Chabotterie (see below), where the capture of General Charette by the Republicans in 1796 marked the end of the long-drawn-out civil war.

Logis de la Chabotterie. To get the most out of your visit you need to do a bit of homework on the Vendean uprising (see page 24) before going round this manor house whose history is inextricably linked to that of the revered Vendean leader Charette. The building, 2.5km south-east of the village, was totally refurbished in time for the 1993 bicentenary of the Vendée wars. Its rooms are now furnished in 18th-century style (almost to "designer" level), its interiors are lit with impeccable taste and ingeniously equipped with recordings of murmuring voices and other background sounds to make you feel you have only just missed actually seeing the occupants. The kitchen contains the very table on which Charette was laid to have his wounds dressed after his capture in the neighbouring woods by General Travot's exultant Republican troops. In the attic you can watch a 12-minute video about Vendean life and the arrest and execution of Charette - by all accounts a dashing and charismatic character.

Afterwards you embark on the 16-minute "Parcours", an atmospheric trail in and out of a series of rooms that display episodes from the events of the 1790s. Though the tableaux and dioramas are excellent, the quality of the French commentary, delivered as if by Charette himself, often suffers from poor acoustics, and the idea of using semi-animated waxworks to "tell" the story is only partly successful. The exhibition space next door holds informative, comprehensive shows on Vendée-war-related themes.

Outside is an immaculately-replanted garden of flowers and vegetables, arranged in geometric borders. You can enjoy strolls and picnics in the large park surrounding the house and follow the "Chemin de Charette" (Charette trail) to find the granite cross that marks the spot where the Vendean general was taken. ▪ Wed-Mon 10am-6pm (15 May-31 Aug, daily 10am-7pm, Fri, Sat until 9pm). Tel : 51 42 81 00. 20F, children free.

Tract' Expo. Open-air display in the village centre of some 50 items of farm equipment from the 1950s, with tractors, threshing-machines and harvesters. ♯ 15-30 June, Sun and public holidays 2.30-6.30pm ; 1 July-15 Sept, daily 2.30-6.30pm. Rue de l'Église (tel : 51 42 80 81). 10F (includes Maison Paysanne - see below).

Maison Paysanne. Guided tours of a small farm cottage, consisting of furnished kitchen, bedroom and attic. Also on display is a collection of "coiffes" or regional headdresses. ♯ 15-30 June, Sun and public holidays 2.30-6.30pm ; 1 July-15 Sept, daily 2.30-6.30pm. Rue de l'Église (tel : 51 42 80 81). 10F (includes tractor museum - see above).

Chapelle de Chêne. Signposted from the roundabout on the D763, just to the southeast of La Chabotterie and about 3km south-east of St-Sulpice, is this curiosity - a tiny chapel in a hollow oak tree. This fairyland-scale place of worship is sandwiched between the roadside and the front garden of a normal house, and has a little porch grafted on to it. ▪

SALIGNY

Pleasant village 21km south-west of Montaigu ; a clue to its claim to fame is the concrete barrow poised outside the Mairie. For the last 10 years a colourful wheelbarrow festival has drawn thousands of spectators every summer to cheer on contestants - whether the serious speed-merchants in the relay race, or the more frivolous fancy-dress-and-decorated-barrow brigade. Prize money totals more than £1,000.

Festival : Course de brouettes (wheelbarrow race), 15 August.

LA SUISSE VENDÉENNE

Strangely, the "Vendean Switzerland" does not take in the Collines Vendéennes (Vendean Hills) but the beautiful valley of the Sèvre Nantaise on the eastern border of the département. At the tourist office of Mortagne-sur-Sèvre you can obtain information on suggested routes through the tranquil lanes of this area, that stretches from Tiffauges in the north to Mallièvre in the south. ■

TIFFAUGES

The substantial ruined castle of "Barbe-bleu" (Bluebeard) - in fact the infamous Gilles de Rais (or Retz) - tower over this little town 20km south-west of Cholet. To recover from the chilling tales of his appalling crimes, you can take pleasant walks by the Sèvre Nantaise river or along miller's tracks and sunken lanes, or set off by car or bicycle on the signposted Circuit de la Suisse Vendéenne (circuit of the Vendean Switzerland, see above) that winds southwards to Mallièvre (see page 90).

Château de Gilles de Rais. When he fought alongside Charles VII and Joan of Arc against the English in the Hundred Years' War, Gilles de Rais (1404-40) seemed set for a glittering military career, reaching the rank of field-marshal at the age of only 25. After the English burnt Joan at the stake for witchcraft in 1431, he retired to his castle at Tiffauges and steadily dissipated his fortune with high living. He turned to alchemy and then, in the belief that he could make gold from the blood of young children, he seized and murdered more than 200 from the areas around his many properties (including the castles of Pornic and Machecoul - see pages 103 and 99) before justice caught up with him and he was hanged and burnt at the stake in Nantes.

Guided tours of the castle - reduced to its present state largely on orders from Cardinal Richelieu more than 300 years ago - take in the Romanesque crypt (site of many terrible deeds) supported by a forest of sturdy columns, the 12th-century keep, the oubliettes (secret dungeons below the round tower, in which prisoners could be "forgotten") and, near the top of the vidame's tower, a whispering gallery with 37 half-moon machicolations (the semi-circular holes in the floor through which missiles could be dropped on invaders). Hold on to small children here, if you don't want them to fall on later arrivals. A route through the spooky corridors of the vidame's tower leads you to a reconstructed laboratory of alchemy.

Within the vast area enclosed by the ruined walls is a magnificent collection of full-sized working reconstructions of 15th-century siege machinery, operated (from May to September) by warriors in medieval costume. To the accompaniment of a witty commentary they load and fire stone cannonballs and large bags of water over 150m distances with great aplomb and offer goggle-eyed children the chance to cross (wooden) swords with them, fire a crossbow or be put in the stocks. ⚔ 1 Apr-30 Nov, Sun & public holidays 2-6pm (1 May-30 Sept, Thurs-Tues 10am-noon & 2-6pm, displays 11am & 3pm, plus 5pm on Sun & public holidays ; 1 July-31 Aug, daily 10am-noon & 2-7pm, displays at 11am, 3pm & 5pm). Tel : 51 65 70 51. 30F, children 15F.

VENDRENNES

Small village on the busy RN160 road 9.5km south-west of Les Herbiers. It is reputed to be the birthplace of the fluffy Vendean "brioche" (a sweet, delicately-flavoured bread), so it is worth buying some here to make comparisons. To the north of the main road you can glimpse the remains of a 12th-century feudal fortress. The Vendean politician and writer Jean Yole (see Soullans, page 41), who wrote novels and essays about the peasant condition, died at the nearby Logis de la Noue in 1956.

Festivals : Fête de la Chasse (game fair), early August.

CHAPTER 6

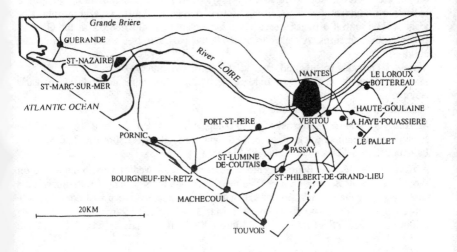

BOURGNEUF-EN-RETZ (Loire-Atlantique)

Village, 33km south-east of the St-Nazaire bridge, on the frontier between Brittany and the Vendée. Bird-lovers should make their way west towards Port du Collet and watch the avocets, egrets and other wading birds congregating nearer and nearer to the shore as the tide rises.

Musée du Pays-de-Retz. Housed in a converted convent opposite the church, the museum shows the history of the region : archaeology, salt-production, folk traditions and regional head-dresses, and some interiors - typical in style, though populated by somewhat effete shop-window mannequins in rustic costume. ♯ Palm Sunday-15 Nov, Sat, Sun 10am-noon & 2-6pm (1 June-30 Sept, Wed-Mon 10am-noon & 2-6pm ; 1 July-31 Aug, daily 10am-noon & 3-7pm). 6 Rue des Moines (tel : 40 21 40 83). 12F, children 6F.

LA GRANDE BRIÈRE (Loire-Atlantique)

The 40,000-hectare nature reserve just to the north of St-Nazaire is surprisingly difficult to get to by car. From the St-Nazaire bridge, take the Nantes direction at the first major intersection and turn off after 4km, at Montoir-de-Bretagne to reach the east side of the park ; if you turn off a little earlier, at Trignac, and have a good map-reader next to you, it is possible to work your way around the west side of this bullrush-fringed peatland wilderness.

The locals, using flat-bottomed boats known as "blins", catch fish and eels and cut reeds for thatching their low, whitewashed cottages. Guided tours of the marshes, full of kingfishers, dragonflies and other wildlife, are available by boat, by horsedrawn cart, on foot or on horseback from the vicinity of villages like St-André-des-Eaux, St-Lyphard, St-Joachim and La Chapelle-des-Marais. Kerhinet, a village on the west side of the park 3.5km south-west of St-Lyphard, has been completely restored, with 18 cottages that house museums, exhibitions and craft workshops. The island of Fédrun on the east side (linked to St-Joachim by a road across the marshes), contains a collection of typical dwellings, lining a circular road, and attracts large numbers of visitors. The tourist offices in each place have plenty of information on the Grande-Brière's other features. A ticket to visit all the park's museums is on sale at 26F, children 13F.

Market : Thursday in July and August, at Kerhinet village.

Festival : Fête de la Brière (marshland festival) at Ste-Anne de St-Joachim, early August.

Specialities : Eels and freshwater fish.

Maison du Sabotier. Clogmaker's workshop, with a video showing the last of the region's craftsmen at work. ♯ 1 April-30 Sept, daily 10am-12.30pm & 2.30-6.30pm. La Chapelle-des-Marais (tel : 40 66 85 01). Free.

Maison de la Mariée. Bouquets, headdresses and other wedding mementoes are on show in a typical Briéron cottage. The nearby village of St-Joachim was renowned a century ago for the manufacture of artificial orange-blossom, worn by brides through- out Europe on their wedding day. ♯ 1 Mar-31 May, daily 9am-12.30pm & 1.30-7.30pm ; 1 June-30 Sept, daily 9am-7.30pm. 130-132 Ile de Fédrun (tel : 40 88 42 04).

GUÉRANDE (Loire-Atlantique)

A charming, entirely walled, medieval town, 20km west of St-Nazaire, whose fortune was founded on the produce of the vast salt marshes that stretch away below it to the west. Although canning, invented in 1809 by the Frenchman Nicolas Appert, eventually proved to be a more convenient way of preserving foodstuffs, many of the "œillets" (salt pans) are still in operation - indeed the white "fleur de sel", the finest grade of local salt, from Guérande is currently much in vogue in British foodie circles.

In the 15th century more than 3,000 people lived within the town's stone boundaries. Today the maze of narrow streets is full of restaurants, crêperies, fascinating craft and antique shops - and tourists. However, since almost all drivers have to park their vehicles outside the ramparts and walk in through one of the four massive gateways, the place enjoys a delightfully hushed atmosphere. The tourist office organises guided walks in the town, and stocks information on other footpaths in the area.

Market : Wednesday and Saturday.

Speciality : Sea-salt.

Musée Régional. The museum of local history is housed in one of the town's massive, 15th-century gatehouses. Furnished interiors give an idea of domestic life on the Guérande peninsula ; other exhibits include porcelain from nearby Le Croisic, paintings, pottery, crafts, and information about the salt and the linen-weaving industries. ⇄ Easter-30 Sept, daily 9.30am-noon & 2-7pm. Porte St-Michel (tel : 40 42 96 52). 16F, children 8F.

Collégiale St-Aubin. If you look up at the tops of the columns supporting this Romanesque/gothic collegiate church you will see that they are carved to represent stories from medieval mythology. Organ concerts are sometimes given during the summer. ▪

Océarium. A 10km drive through the marshes to the south-west of Guérande takes you to an attractive fishing port where you can visit one of Europe's latest aquariums. Built in the shape of a starfish, it incorporates an 11m tunnel through which you can wander, surrounded by hundreds of Atlantic fish. ⇄ 1 Feb-31 Dec, daily 10am-noon & 2-7pm (1-30 June, daily 10am-7pm ; 1 July-31 Aug, daily 10am-11pm). Avenue de St-Goustan, Le Croisic (tel : 40 23 02 44). 42F, children 26F.

Musée des Marais Salants. The salt industry explained in the village of Batz-sur-Mer, 8km south-west of Guérande. A video shows how the residue of salt is created from allowing seawater to evaporate in the large, rectangular salt pans ; pictures, tools, clothes and furniture give an idea of the saltworkers' way of life. ▪ Sat, Sun 3-7pm (1 June-30 Sept, daily 10am-noon & 3-7pm). 29bis Rue Pasteur, Batz-sur-Mer (tel : 40 23 82 79). 16F, children 10F.

Château de Careil. Just off the D92, 4km south of Guérande, is a handsome 14th-century fortress with Renaissance additions that is still, in part, a private home. A half-hour guided tour leads through a series of immense rooms with magnificent timber ceilings that were formerly occupied by the soldiers garrisoned here. Twice weekly during July and August you can visit the castle by candlelight, but be sure to arrive promptly as there is only one tour each evening. ⇄ 1 Apr-31 May, daily 3-6pm ; 1 June-1 Oct, daily 10.30am-noon & 2.30-6pm (1 July-31 Aug, candlelight tours Wed, Sat 9.30pm). Tel : 40 60 22 99. 10F.

La Baule. For a sophisticated day at the seaside, take a trip to this fashionable Breton resort 6km to the south of Guérande. Luxury hotels, apartment buildings and restaurants, interspersed with occasional reminders of the town's 19th-century origins in the form of early seaside bourgeois houses, line the 5km-long promenade that sweeps around the beautiful sandy bay. ▪

HAUTE-GOULAINE (Loire-Atlantique)

The marshes surrounding this village 7km south-east of Nantes, once supplied frog's legs for local tables (though this delicacy is now more likely to be imported, deep-frozen, from countries like Malaysia).

Château de Goulaine. Guided tours of a handsome castle - still in the hands of the de Goulaine family after more than 1,000 years - where the French kings Henri IV and, later, Louis XIV are reputed to have stayed. A century ago one of the family's cooks created "beurre-blanc", the wonderful, buttery sauce that accompanies so many fish dishes in the Nantes region.

The estate is celebrated for the Marquis de Goulaine wine, a Muscadet de Sèvre-et-Maine produced from the vineyards that stretch out around the house, which you have a chance to sample and buy. During the warmer months you can also visit a tropical butterfly house that leans against the outer walls. ♯ Easter-31 Oct ; Sat, Sun & bank holidays 2-6pm (15 June-15 Sept, Wed-Mon 2-6pm). Tèl : 40 54 91 42. 20F (25F includes wine-tasting).

LA HAYE-FOUASSIERE (Loire-Atlantique)

Small village 16km south-east of Nantes, known for "fouasse" (sometimes written "fouace") - a type of sweet bread like a rather compact brioche. The tasty tradition is extended today, since the village also has an ultra-modern factory turning out quantities of biscuits under the LU label (from Lefèvre-Utile, one of the great Nantes biscuit companies).

Specialities : Muscadet, Gros-Plant and Coteaux d'Ancenis wines, fouasse, LU biscuits.

Maison des Vins de Nantes. Surrounded by the vineyards of the Muscadet region (that, alone, produce 85 million bottles a year), this is where you can learn all about sharp, white Gros-Plant, the light wines of the Coteaux d'Ancenis, and the three types of Muscadet : those of the Coteaux de la Loire, of Sèvre-et-Maine, and that of the central area south of Nantes. ▪ Mon-Fri 8.30am-12.30pm & 1.30-6.30pm (1 June-30 Sept, daily 9.30am-12.30pm & 1.30-6.30pm). Closed on public holidays. Tel : 40 36 90 10. Free.

LE LOROUX-BOTTEREAU (Loire-Atlantique)

It is possible to rent boats for a tour of the marshes at this village, 18km east of Nantes.

Église de St-Jean-Baptiste. On the north wall of the church, beneath an 18th-century bas-relief of Moses and the Israelites, are fixed a pair of interesting frescoes rescued from an earlier church in the village. Dating from around 1200, they are thought to show episodes from the life of St Giles - a Greek who settled in France in the area of Nîmes.

The top picture is a hunting scene, recalling a legend that King Flavius of the Goths once tried to shoot a deer which was under the saint's protection ; the lower one is said to depict St Giles receiving the confession of the Emperor Charlemagne that he had made his own sister pregnant - the left-hand side of the picture shows the girl, Gisèle, being married off to a nobleman.

You can climb to the top of the tower for a superb view over the surrounding vineyards (key obtainable from the tourist office). ▪

MACHECOUL (Loire-Atlantique)

This busy, attractive market town on the edge of the Marais Breton is dominated by the twin spires of its large 19th-century church and lies on the border of the Vendée and Loire-Atlantique, 40km south-west of Nantes. Leading from the 19th-century market hall is Rue du Marché, lined with interesting shops and paintwork-scraping concrete bollards that look like giant cannonballs. From behind clumps of trees along the banks of the river Falleron rises, like a jagged tooth, the silhouette of the ruined castle that once belonged to the sadistic Gilles de Rais (see Tiffauges, page 94 and St-Étienne-de-Mer-Morte, page 37).

At the start of the Vendée wars the town saw one of the first risings against the Republicans when, on 11 March 1793, 3,000 Vendeans massacred those whose sympathies lay with the new regime (see page 25).

Today, as well as market-gardening, Machecoul's thriving businesses include the Séguin distillery and a factory making Gitane bicycles. There are several signposted footpaths and cycle trails, and you can rent bikes from the tourist office at Place du Port. Don't miss a trip around the marshes to the west - by car, bike, canoe or on foot (see Port-La-Roche, page 32).

Market : Wednesday.

Specialities : Séguin eau-de-vie (see below), cheeses from Fromagerie Beillevaire, "mâche" (winter leaves known as lamb's lettuce or corn salad), "muguet" (lilies-of-the-valley, popular throughout France as a 1 May gift).

Distillerie Séguin. Tastings of the various products feature during a 45-minute guided tour of this distillery. Its best-known creation is the brandy-like eau-de-vie "Fine Bretagne", created from wines of the Coteaux de la Loire, and matured for seven years in oak barrels. ♯ 1 July-31 Aug, Mon-Fri ; first tour 2pm, last tour 4.15pm. 10 Boulevard St-Rémy (tel : 40 31 40 51).

NANTES (Loire-Atlantique)

Shipbuilding, biscuit-manufacturing, sugar-refining and food-canning are the livelihoods of this pleasant river port of 250,000 inhabitants, straddling the Loire, that grew rich in the 17th and 18th centuries - largely on the proceeds of the sugar and slave trades. During the Wars of the Vendée it was the site of a ferocious battle, where the Vendean leader Cathelineau was mortally wounded, and later the headquarters for the notorious Republican General Carrier who instituted the horrific drownings of prisoners in the Loire. The town was heavily bombed by the Allies in 1943, though you would not guess it from the profusion of old buildings, some dating back to the Middle Ages.

The big-city atmosphere comes as something of a shock after you have spent a tranquil week or two buried in the Vendean countryside. To get the best out of a day trip, you should try and visit between Wednesday and Saturday - too many shops are closed on Mondays, and most museums are shut on Tuesdays (and also on public holidays). Driving can be a headache, as the one-way systems are confusing. Car parks are signposted from an inner ring road called "Circuit coeur", but easy-to-spot ones include a multi-storey car park beneath the Tour de Bretagne - a skyscraper that you can see from almost anywhere in town - and another near the railway station, or you could try the suburban streets around the edge. A less stressful alternative is to travel in by train, leaving the platform by the "sortie nord" which brings you out on the north side opposite the tram station and the Jardin des Plantes (see below), ready to start exploring. The city's brand-new tramway system has one east-west route and another running north-south. Tickets, costing around 7F, are valid for an hour; day-tickets 17F.

A good first stop is the tourist office in Place du Commerce, where you can start by picking up a town plan and browsing through the brochures. Just to the south, across the tram tracks, is the attractive "Ile Feydeau" (Feydeau island) area, fused with the mainland only since the 1930s. The narrow, central street of the former island, Rue Kervégan, is lined with the houses of 18th-century shipowners and embellished by ornate balconies and carved stone decoration over doors and windows.

On the north side of Place du Commerce is Passage Pommeraye, an unusual, 19th-century shopping arcade, with shops on different levels, linked by decorated steps that rise steeply to finish at Rue Crébillon (a smart street where you come across many of the town's best shops). Farther north, on Rue du Calvaire, you will find Galeries Lafayette department store ; the familiar sight of Marks and Spencer is close by, and even Habitat on Rue de Budapest. If, on the other hand, you turn south-west on Rue Crébillon you come to Place Graslin and, just beyond the beautiful, turn-of-the-century brasserie called La Cigale, an elegant, traffic-free avenue of 18th-century houses known as Cours Cambronne.

The picturesque, pedestrianised streets around the Église Ste-Croix, to the east of the central Cours des 50 Otages, contain several 15th- and 16th-century houses and many unusual, specialist shops.

Markets : Rue Talensac & Place du Bouffay, Tues-Sun ; Place du Ralliement, Wednesday ; Place Ste-Anne, Thursday ; Place de la Petite-Hollande, Saturday.

Flea market : Place Viarme, Saturday.

Festivals : Carnival, March ; International summer festival of world music, July; Festival of the Atlantic (music), July.

Specialities : Beurre-blanc nantais (a rich, buttery sauce to accompany fish), Berlingots nantais (pyramid-shaped boiled sweets), canard nantais (duck), biscuits (BN and Belin brands), sugar refined by Béghin-Say, market-gardening - especially carrots, leeks, and muguet (lilies-of-the-valley, traditionally purchased throughout France on 1 May).

Musée du Château des Ducs de Bretagne. The majestic castle, lying between the Ile Feydeau and the railway station, was the residence of the dukes of Brittany and kings of France. Today it contains an interesting folk museum, with solid pieces of Breton furniture and a collection of regional pottery, and the Musée des Salorges which deals with the commercial and industrial history of Nantes over the last two centuries. ▪ Wed-Mon 10am-noon & 2-6pm (1 July-31 Aug, daily 10am-noon & 2-6pm. Cours John-Kennedy (tel : 40 41 56 56). Castle and both museums 30F, children 15F (free on Sundays).

Cathédrale St-Pierre et St-Paul. The flamboyant-gothic cathedral is of comparatively recent date. Within the lofty, white stone interior is the spectacularly decorated tomb of Duke François II of Brittany and his wife, commissioned by their daughter, Anne of Brittany, in 1502. ▪ Daily 8.30am-7pm (crypt Mon-Sat 10am-12.30pm & 2-5pm, Sun 2-6pm). Place St-Pierre. Free.

Musée des Beaux-Arts. Western painting from the 13th century to the present, including some fine works by Georges de la Tour, a strong showing of 19th-century French artists and a large collection of abstract and contemporary art that includes 11 works by Kandinsky. Do not miss the unusual sight of an immense Rubens hanging above the gloomy, subterranean lavatories. ▪ Wed-Mon 10am-noon & 1-5.45pm. 10 Rue Georges-Clemenceau (tel : 40 41 65 65). 20F, children 10F (free on Sundays).

Jardin des Plantes. The city's delightful botanical gardens that lie opposite the railway station have medicinal plants, several ponds, and wonderful spring displays of magnolias, camellias and rhododendrons. ■ Daily 8am-dusk (greenhouses closed on Tuesdays). Free.

Muséum d'Histoire Naturelle. Classic natural history museum, full of stuffed animals and skeletons of every description. The most unexpected aspect is a vivarium housing a gigantic live python, scorpions, stick-insects, toads and other creatures. ■ Tues-Sat 10am-noon & 2-6pm, Sun 2-6pm. 12 Rue Voltaire (tel : 40 41 67 67). 20F, children 10F (free on Sundays).

Musée Dobrée. Thomas Dobrée (1810-95), son of a rich Nantes shipowner, built this granite palace to house his collections of furniture, prints, enamels, oriental porcelain, sculpture and curiosities that include the heart of Anne, the 15th-century queen of Brittany who became twice queen of France (by marrying Charles VIII and, later, Louis XII). ■ Tues-Sun 10am-noon & 1.30-5.30pm. Rue Voltaire (tel : 40 71 03 50). 20F, children 10F (free on Sundays).

Pavillon Madeleine Lilas. An enchanting concept, showing more than 15 miniature scenes of 20th-century life as if they were episodes from that of the imaginary Madeleine and her family. Based on an extensive collection of Dinky-type model cars, it uses superb décors, lighting and sound effects to re-create cheerful family outings and historical events. Picnics in the Bois de Boulogne, a trip to the seaside, famous moments from the First and Second World Wars, and an amazingly faithful reconstruction of a street scene from the Paris riots of 1968 are all viewed at eye-level through glass windows. An explanatory brochure is available in English. Other attractions include a miniature train, and videos to amuse younger children. The museum is still expanding, and will be adding new scenes each year. Temporary exhibitions on 20th-century themes are given in a large warehouse next-door. ■ Wed-Mon 10.30am-6pm. 10 Rue Meuris (tel : 40 71 85 00). 40F, students 30F, children 25F (family ticket 100F) ; supplement for temporary exhibitions.

Musée de la Poupée et des Jouets Anciens. Unprepossessing from the outside, this delightful Victorian house is crammed with dolls and toys of every description scrutinising visitors through hundreds of pairs of glassy eyes. Tiny tables are laid for tea with mini crockery from great names like Lunéville and Gien ; upstairs are English and French dolls'-houses, and cupboards crammed with playing-cards and traditional games like the "Jeu de l'Oie" (the Goose Game) - as familiar to French children as "Snakes & Ladders" is to the British. ♯ 15 Oct-15 Apr, Wed-Sun 2.30-5.30pm ; 15 Apr-15 Sept, Wed-Sat 2.30-5.30pm. 39 Boulevard St-Aignan (tel : 40 69 14 41). 20F, children 10F

Musée Jules Verne. Although he was born in Nantes, the great visionary writer never actually lived in this late-19th-century house overlooking the river. The collection of different editions of his many works would interest serious students, but is not guaranteed to thrill children as it has a distinctly "glass-case" feel to it. The only sparks of life are some of the spin-offs from "Around the World in 80 Days" that include magic-lantern slides and puzzles, a small room-setting using Verne's own furniture, and a cosily-carpeted spacecraft complete with a stuffed dog. ■ Wed-Mon 10am-12.30pm & 2-5pm. 3 Rue de l'Hermitage (tel : 40 69 72 52). 8F, children 4F

"Maillé-Brezé": escorteur d'escadre. You can scramble over a 1950s French destroyer, bristling with rocket- and missile-launchers, that is now moored on the Loire as a floating museum. ■ Wed, Sat, Sun, 2-5pm (1 Apr-30 Sept, Wed-Mon 2-5pm). Quai de la Fosse (tel : 40 69 56 82). 25F, children 10F

Tour de Bretagne. Enjoy a fantastic, near-aerial view from the top of the city's tallest building. ▪ Mon-Fri 12.15-1.45pm, Sat 1.15-4.45pm. Cours des 50 Otages. Free.

L'Erdre et ses Châteaux. You can take a two-hour cruise along the breathtakingly beautiful river Erdre, to the north of Nantes, aboard rather grotesque, glass-sided boats (fortunately you can't see them once you're on board). The trip, with commentary, takes you along this peaceful waterway which is lined with green fields and decorated with country mansions dating from Renaissance times. ♯ 1 Apr-30 Nov ; timetable from tourist offices. Bateaux Nantais, Quai de la Motte Rouge, Place Waldeck-Rousseau (tel : 40 14 51 14). 50F, children 25F ; ▪ Three-hour lunch and dinner cruises (advance booking essential) 235F & 265F, children 180F & 180F.

LE PALLET (Loire-Atlantique)

Village 20km south-east of Nantes, that was the birthplace of the 12th-century philosopher and theologian Pierre Abélard who fell in love with, and secretly married, his young pupil Héloïse. Once the scandalous affair became known, she entered a convent from which she wrote him a series of celebrated love-letters. He, suffering intense persecution, became first a monk and then a hermit before taking up the post of abbot at a monastery in Brittany. Héloïse died 22 years after Abélard, in 1164, and was buried beside him.

There are signposted walks around the village, rock-climbing at the nearby village of La Rochelle, and boats for hire on the Sèvre Nantaise river.

Musée du Vignoble de Nantes. This museum, in a former chapel, shows local traditions connected with wine production, tells the history of the village, the life and times of Abélard, and describes the career of the botanist Barrin de la Galissonnière, governor of Quebec under Louis XV, who was responsible for introducing many rare trees into the district. ♯ Easter to 1 Nov ; Sat, Sun & public holidays 2.30-6.30pm (15 June-15 Sept, Tues-Sun 2.30-6.30pm). Tel : 40 80 40 24. 10F, children 3F.

Chapelle Ste-Anne. Romanesque chapel on the site of Abélard's castle ; nearby is a fine view over the Sèvre Nantaise river. ▪

Monnières church. In the village on the opposite side of the river, you can see depictions of vines and wine in the modern stained-glass windows that decorate the 15th-century church. ▪

PASSAY (Loire-Atlantique)

Fishing village on the eastern edge of the Lac de Grand-Lieu, 17km south of Nantes. Only if you arrive at Nantes by plane have you a chance to appreciate the vastness of this 6,300-hectare lake, the area of which literally doubles in the wet winter months. Long, black-netting eel-traps lie on the flat, rush-fringed shores, while nearby float sinister, tarred boxes, like miniature wartime landing-craft, where the catches are stored. Visitors are allowed to penetrate the interior of this mysterious wetland (a wildlife reserve that is an important staging-post for migrating birds and holds Europe's largest heron colony of more than 1,000 pairs) on only two occasions a year - 15 August, and the following Sunday. On these days, if you turn up before 8.30am, you can accompany the 15 local fishermen on a 1½-hour trip into the interior by "plate" (flat-bottomed boat) through the reeds and water-lilies, wading into the water to help pull in the long "senne" nets full of fish. The catch is sold off in aid of fishermen's charities.

Market : Wednesday, at La Chevrolière (3km to the east).

Saillier Michaël

Festivals : Fête des Anguilles (eel festival), mid-April. Fête de la Pêche (fishing festival), 15 August and following Sunday.
Speciality : Eels.

Maison du Pêcheur. A lighthouse-like observatory towers over the village, marking the position of this museum of local life among the low, whitewashed fishermen's cottages. From the top you can look through telescopes at the distant lake, or watch the wildlife on a television monitor which shows live pictures from a camera installed several kilometres away. Most interesting is the museum itself, at the far end of the garden. Large wall-panels carry explanations about the fragile ecosystem of this watery environment ; there are displays showing local fishing equipment and, as the grand finale, a wonderful aquarium of eels, carp, pike and other freshwater fish. ■ Daily 10am-noon & 3-6.30pm. 16 Rue Yves-Brisson (tel: 40 31 36 46). 12F, children 6F.

PORNIC (Loire-Atlantique)

There is a real Breton flavour to this chic resort, 18km south of the St-Nazaire bridge, that was a favourite of Gustave Flaubert, George Sand and other literary celebrities during the last century. The rocky coastline is dominated by a fairy-tale castle with pointed, slate roofs, whose prettiness belies the fact that it once belonged to the infamous Gilles de Rais (see St-Étienne-de-Mer-Morte, page 37 and Tiffauges, page 94). Some 900 yachts and cruisers bob in the marina below.

The Grande Randonnée de la Côte de Jade - a long-distance trail that uses an old Customs path - runs north and south along the coast ; another, the GR du Pays de Retz, wanders inland through the gently rolling countryside. If you ramble north - or even drive up the D213 - past the seaside town of St-Michel-Chef-Chef 8km north of Pornic, be sure to breathe deeply as you come abreast of it to catch the wonderful smell of baking (it will even reach your nostrils in the car, if you wind down the window). The town is the home of the St-Michel biscuit factory, whose products you will find in rows on supermarket shelves.

Dolmen des Mousseaux. Double funeral chamber to the west of Pornic, signposted from the beach near the castle. It is thought to date from 3500BC. ▪

Ferme de la Douce-Vie. There is something of a Wild West flavour to the idea of trips by horse-drawn cart around a bison farm. If you want to see what the meat tastes like, you can telephone to book a meal at this "ferme-auberge" (farm-restaurant) 4km north-east of Pornic, where bison or the farm's other home-raised product, pork, often feature on the menu. * 1 July-31 Aug, daily 2-7pm. Clion-sur-Mer (tel : 40 64 86 67). 30F, children 25F.

PORT-ST-PERE (Loire-Atlantique)

Village 16km south-west of Nantes, near the north-western corner of the Lac de Grand-Lieu.

Safari Africain. Thatched mud huts add to the African atmosphere at this safari park 2km south-west of the village, where you can see lions, giraffes, flamingos and other non-indigenous creatures. ⧢ Mid Feb-mid Nov, daily 9am-7pm. Port-St-Père (tel : 40 04 82 82). 65F, children 35F.

La Métairie d'Ardennes. Hire a canoe and paddle up the river Tenu or, if you want to make a day of it, farther still along the Acheneau from an attractively restored farmhouse near the wildlife reserve of Grand-Lieu, 5km south of Port-St-Père. ⧢ 1 May-30 Sept, daily. Ardennes, near Ste-Pazanne (tel : 40 02 77 16).

ST-LUMINE-DE-COUTAIS (Loire-Atlantique)

About 30km south-west of Nantes as the heron flies, this small village on the edge of the Lac de Grand-Lieu offers a spectacular view of the lake and surrounding villages from the top of its 40m-high church tower. A strange custom takes place on 14 July each year when a procession follows "le cheval Mallet" (a wooden hobby-horse rather like those seen in West Country May-Day celebrations in Britain). You can see an audio-visual description of this traditional event near to the village's museum.
Festival : Le Cheval Mallet (hobby-horse procession), 14 July.

Musée d'art sacré. Guided tour of a museum of relics, banners, chalices, and other examples of religious art, in a picturesque 16th-century chapel. * 1 July-31 Aug, daily 10am-noon & 3-7pm. Tel : 40 02 90 25. 4F.

ST-MARC-SUR-MER (Loire-Atlantique)

A seaside village, 11km south-west of St-Nazaire, that is a place of pilgrimage for fans of the French actor-director Jacques Tati. Devotees can have fun trying to spot the locations used in the charming 1953 film "Les vacances de Monsieur Hulot" - the beachside hotel building still stands, but has become a block of flats.
The French seem mystified by the British reverence for Tati's comic hero ; they are more likely to be able to quote chunks of some Ealing comedy than to remember a frame of the Hulot film. ▪

ST-NAZAIRE (Loire-Atlantique)

Cross the beautiful, curved 3.35km bridge - the longest in France when it was built in 1975 (toll 30F each way at the time of writing, but due to be toll-free from late 1995) - and you see beneath you the rooftops change from south-of-the-Loire Roman tiles to the more businesslike slate of Brittany. A heavily-fortified German U-boat port during the Second World War - the submarine base was the target of a 1942 Anglo-Canadian commando raid - 85 per cent of St-Nazaire was flattened by Allied bombing, and has been entirely rebuilt since. Its shipbuilding industry continues to dominate the northern shore of the Loire estuary.

Écomusée et visite du sous-marin "Espadon". If you telephone ahead to book a precise time, you can set foot on a real French submarine (albeit a 1950s model). Picking you way on foot over the ropes and cables slung around the water's edge near the war-time submarine pens, you cannot refrain from shuddering when you catch your first glimpse of the "Espadon's" sinister silhouette, as she floats in the impregnable German-built, concrete-roofed submarine lock. An enthusiastic ex-submariner takes groups of 15 round, up and down the narrow companionways and steep ladders (ladies would be well advised to wear trousers), cheerfully describing life aboard when there were bunks for only two-thirds of the crew, and just two lavatories for the 65 men aboard. It's all in French, but you can ask for an English text to read up on the details. Afterwards, to shake off claustrophobia, you can climb to the terrace on top of the lock's roof for a view over the river, town and dockyards.

After the submarine, the Écomusée is a bit of an anticlimax. It contains information on birdlife, the shipbuilding industry (including some splendid models), prisms from a lighthouse, and photographs of the wartime destruction of the town and its reconstruction (many inhabitants lived for 30 years in pre-fabricated buildings). ▪ Museum : Wed-Mon 10am-noon & 2-6pm (1 June-15 Sept, daily 9.30am-7pm), Rue du Bac de Mindin (tel : 40 66 79 66) ; 15F, children 10F. Submarine : Wed & Sun 10am-noon & 2-6pm (15 Mar-31 Oct, Wed-Sun 10am-noon & 2-6pm ; 1 June-12 Sept, daily 9.30am-6.30pm) ; booking tel : 40 22 35 33 ; 40F, children 15F (includes Écomusée).

ST-PHILBERT-DE-GRAND-LIEU (Loire-Atlantique)

In this pretty village 23km south of Nantes, near the southern limit of the great wetland known as the Lac de Grand-Lieu, stands one of the oldest churches in the whole of France (see below). You can rent boats from about 35F an hour, or fish in the calm waters of the Boulogne river ; opposite the campsite just to the north of the river is a cheery playground equipped with bouncy castles, mini-golf and other delights.

Market : Sunday.

Specialities : Muscadet and Gros-Plant wines.

Brocante : St-Philbert Brocante, La Chaussée (on the northern edge of the village, just before the D117). Thurs-Tues 10am-1pm & 2.30-7pm.

Abbatiale St-Philbert. More than 20,000 people come every year to visit this ancient Carolingian abbey church. In 815 the monks from St Philbert's Abbey on the island of Noirmoutier, fleeing from Norman invasion, built the church to hold the relics of their saint. Within its simple exterior, the decoration is a harmonious mixture of alternating bands of white stone and warm brick. You can see the sarcophagus in the crypt, though St Philbert's remains were removed as long ago as 858, and are now at Tournus in Burgundy. Concerts and exhibitions in summer. ▪

Maison de l'Avifaune du Lac. Museum devoted to more than 200 types of bird that live near or pass through the great wetland to the north. As well as an audio-visual presentation about the flora and fauna of the Lac de Grand-Lieu, you can see live television pictures of the lake. ▪ Tues-Sun 9.30am-12.30pm & 2-5pm (1 Apr-30 Sept,

Tues-Sun 10am-noon & 3-6.30pm). Entrance via tourist office, Rue de l'Abreuvoir (tel : 40 78 73 88). 11F

TOUVOIS (Loire-Atlantique)

Village 40km south of Nantes, that was on the old pilgrim route to Santiago de Compostela (see page 20).

Market : Second and fourth Mondays of the month.

Maison du Paysan. Tools and other artefacts give an idea of the way of life in the surrounding agricultural and winemaking area. ♯ 15 June-15 Sept ; Wed, Sat, Sun 2.30-6.30pm. (Tel : 40 31 64 05). 10F

Chapelle de Fréligné. The delicate spire visible across a field, 2km south of Touvois, tempts you to stop and explore this 12th-century chapel. Said to have been built by English sea-captains returning from the Crusades, it was severely damaged by fire during the Wars of the Vendée and has been much restored since. Nearby, on the Touvois side of the village, is the site of ferocious fighting that left 1,200 Republican soldiers and 400 Vendeans dead. The little garden across the way from the battle site is the centre for a pilgrimage in early September. ▪

VERTOU (Loire-Atlantique)

Riverside village lying just off the south-east side of the expressway that hurtles around Nantes. You can hire boats here to explore the Sèvre Nantaise river on your own, or be taken on a guided tour (see below) on something larger.

La Sèvre romantique. One-hour cruises, with commentary, on the picturesque Sèvre Nantaise river, passing through the Muscadet vineyards. ♯ Easter-30 Sept ; timetable from tourist offices. Embarcadère Bateaux Nantais, Parc de la Sèvre et du Loiry (tel : 40 14 51 14). 30F, children 20F

INDEX

Achevé d'imprimer
en mars 1997
sur les presses de
l'Imprimerie Graphique de l'Ouest
au Poiré-sur-Vie
(Vendée)

Dépôt légal : mars 1997

Imprimé en France